WILDLIFE and PLANTS of the world

An updated and expanded edition of *Wildlife of the World*

now including plants, microorganisms, and biomes

Volume 3

Marshall Cavendish
New York • London • Toronto • Sydney

Marshall Cavendish Corporation
99 White Plains Road
Tarrytown, New York 10591-9001

Created by **Brown Partworks Ltd**

Library of Congress Cataloging-in-Publication Data

Wildlife and plants of the world.
    p.   cm.
    Includes bibliographical references and index.
    Summary: Alphabetically-arranged illustrated articles introduce over 350 animals, plants, and habitats and efforts to protect them.
    ISBN 0-7614-7099-9 (set : lib. bdg. : alk. paper)
    1. Animals—Juvenile literature. 2. Plants—Juvenile literature.
[1. Animals. 2. Plants.] I. Marshall Cavendish Corporation.
QL49.W539   1998
578—DC21   97-32139
                                 CIP
                                 AC

ISBN 0-7614-7099-9 (set)
ISBN 0-7614-7102-2 (vol.3)

Printed in Malaysia
Bound in the United States

Brown Packaging

Editorial consultants:
        • Joshua Ginsberg, Ph.D.
        • Jefferey Kaufmann, Ph.D.
        • Paul Sieswerda, Ph.D.
          (Wildlife Conservation Society)
        • Special thanks to the Dept. of Botany,
          The Natural History Museum, U.K.

Editors:	Deborah Evans
	Leon Gray
Assistant editor:	Amanda Harman
Art editors:	Joan Curtis
	Alison Gardner
	Sandra Horth
Picture researchers:	Amanda Baker
	Brenda Clynch
Illustrations:	Bill Botten
	John Francis

Marshall Cavendish Corporation

Editorial director:	Paul Bernabeo
Project editor:	Debra M. Jacobs
Editorial consultant:	Elizabeth Kaplan

PICTURE CREDITS

The publishers would like to thank Natural History Photographic Agency, Ardingly, Sussex, U.K., for supplying the following pictures:

Agence Nature 152, 190; Bryan & Cherry Alexander 151, 189; A.N.T. (Bruce Thomson) 144, 186; Bill Bachmann 183; J. & M. Bain 156; Anthony Bannister 180, 181, 184; Alan P. Barnes 134; G. I. Bernard 172; Joe B. Blossom 171, 182; Laurie Campbell 157; James H. Carmichael Jr. 137; Karin Cianelli 173; Stephen Dalton 139, 140, 141, 160, 161, 185; Manfred Danegger 162, 163; Robert J. Erwin 167; K. Ghani 187; Jeff Goodman 188; Brian Hawkes 159; Hellio & Van Ingen 158; Stephen Krasemann 136, 165, 170, 177; Michael Leach 142, 145, 174; Lutra 153, 154; Trevor McDonald 179; Rod Planck 138; Dr. Ivan Polunin 155, 175; Steve Robinson 168, 169; Jany Sauvanet 147; Phillipa Scott 143; John Shaw 148, 149, 150, 166, 178; Mark Wellard 176; Martin Wendler 146.

Additional pictures supplied by:
Oxford Scientific Films 164.

Front cover
Main image: Emerald swallowtail butterfly, photographed by Alan P. Barnes.
Additional image: Giant saguaro cactus, photographed by Rod Planck.

Status

In the Key Facts on the species described in this publication, you will find details of the appearance, name (both Latin and common name wherever possible), breeding habits, and so on. The status of an organism indicates how common it is. The status of each organism is based on reference works prepared by two organizations: *1996 IUCN Red List of Threatened Animals* published by the International Union for Conservation of Nature and Natural Resources (IUCN) and *Endangered and Threatened Wildlife and Plants* published in 1997 by the United States Government Printing Office (USGPO)

Extinct:	No sighting in the last 40 years
Endangered:	In danger of becoming extinct
Threatened:	A species that will become endangered if its present condition in the wild continues to deteriorate
Rare:	Not threatened, but not frequently found in the wild
In captivity:	A species that is extinct in the wild but has been kept successfully in captivity
Feral:	Animals that have been domesticated and have escaped into the wild
Common:	Frequently found within its range, which may be limited
Widespread:	Commonly found in many parts of the world

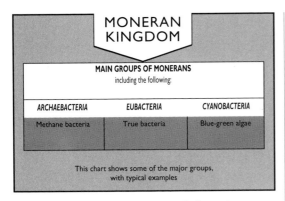

MONERAN KINGDOM

MAIN GROUPS OF MONERANS including the following:		
ARCHAEBACTERIA	**EUBACTERIA**	**CYANOBACTERIA**
Methane bacteria	True bacteria	Blue-green algae

This chart shows some of the major groups, with typical examples

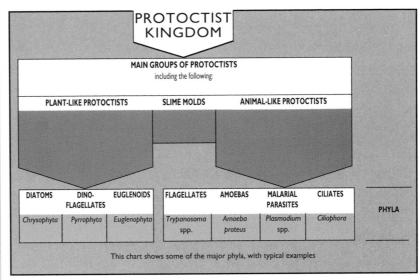

PROTOCTIST KINGDOM

MAIN GROUPS OF PROTOCTISTS including the following:							
PLANT-LIKE PROTOCTISTS			**SLIME MOLDS**	**ANIMAL-LIKE PROTOCTISTS**			
DIATOMS	**DINO-FLAGELLATES**	**EUGLENOIDS**		**FLAGELLATES**	**AMOEBAS**	**MALARIAL PARASITES**	**CILIATES**
Chrysophyta	*Pyrrophyta*	*Euglenophyta*		*Trypanosoma* spp.	*Amoeba proteus*	*Plasmodium* spp.	*Ciliophora*

PHYLA

This chart shows some of the major phyla, with typical examples

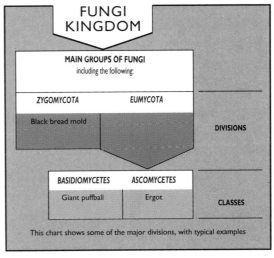

FUNGI KINGDOM

MAIN GROUPS OF FUNGI including the following:	
ZYGOMYCOTA	**EUMYCOTA**
Black bread mold	

DIVISIONS

BASIDIOMYCETES	**ASCOMYCETES**
Giant puffball	Ergot

CLASSES

This chart shows some of the major divisions, with typical examples

COLOR GUIDE

MONERANS, PROTOCTISTS, & FUNGI

Moneran, protoctist, and fungi kingdoms

Three groups of living things are not classified in the animal and plant kingdoms. These are the moneran, protoctist, and fungi kingdoms. Monerans are tiny, single-celled organisms that have no distinct nucleus. The nucleus is the control center of the cell. In contrast, protoctists and fungi have visibly distinct nuclei and tiny organs (called organelles). However, classification is a topic for much debate, and many scientists disagree on the classification of organisms in these three kingdoms.

The moneran kingdom contains all the microscopic, single-celled organisms that do not have distinct nuclei. The three main groups of monerans are: true bacteria, blue-green algae, and methane bacteria. The largest group of monerans is the true bacteria (*Eubacteria*).

For over a billion years, bacteria were the only living things on the earth. Then about 1.5 billion years ago, new organisms, called protoctists (formerly known as protists), evolved from the methane bacteria. All protoctists are single-celled organisms, but their cell structure is more complex than monerans. For example, protoctists have nuclei.

Scientists tend to classify an organism as a protoctist when they cannot place the organism in the animal, plant, or fungi kingdoms. Protoctists are grouped into phyla that have animal-, plant-, or fungus-like features. Single-celled algae, such as diatoms and euglenoids, behave like plants. Amoebas can move about and are more like animals. Slime molds form a subkingdom that have characteristics similar to the fungi kingdom.

Fungi make up the last kingdom of living things. Mushrooms, toadstools, and molds are all fungi. Fungi differ from animals and plants in that they depend on other organisms for their food. Like plants, fungi form groups called divisions. There are two divisions in the fungi kingdom.

See Volume 17 for more information on monerans, protoctists, and fungi.

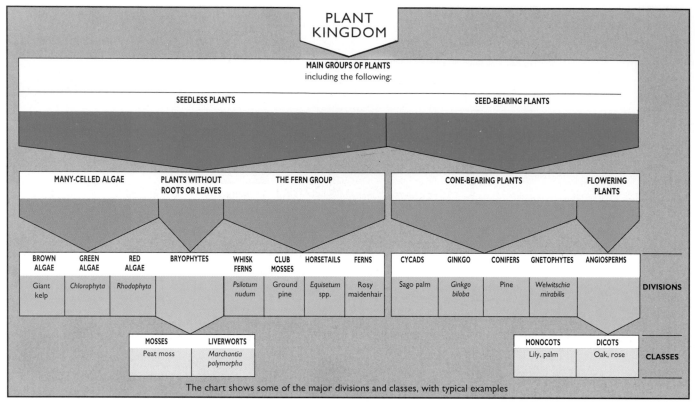

PLANT KINGDOM

MAIN GROUPS OF PLANTS
including the following:

SEEDLESS PLANTS	SEED-BEARING PLANTS

MANY-CELLED ALGAE	PLANTS WITHOUT ROOTS OR LEAVES	THE FERN GROUP	CONE-BEARING PLANTS	FLOWERING PLANTS

BROWN ALGAE	GREEN ALGAE	RED ALGAE	BRYOPHYTES	WHISK FERNS	CLUB MOSSES	HORSETAILS	FERNS	CYCADS	GINKGO	CONIFERS	GNETOPHYTES	ANGIOSPERMS	**DIVISIONS**
Giant kelp	*Chlorophyta*	*Rhodophyta*		*Psilotum nudum*	Ground pine	*Equisetum* spp.	Rosy maidenhair	Sago palm	*Ginkgo biloba*	Pine	*Welwitschia mirabilis*		

MOSSES	LIVERWORTS	MONOCOTS	DICOTS	**CLASSES**
Peat moss	*Marchantia polymorpha*	Lily, palm	Oak, rose	

The chart shows some of the major divisions and classes, with typical examples

The plant kingdom

Every plant, from the tiniest shrub to the tallest tree, belongs to the plant kingdom. There are about 500,000 different kinds (species) of plant that have been identified.

The plant kingdom (shown above) can be divided into 13 divisions. A plant division is similar to a phylum in animal classification. Each division represents a number of classes of plants that all have certain features in common.

The simplest plants are algae, all of which live in water. This set of books classifies three divisions of multicellular (or many-celled) algae in the plant kingdom. Some scientists, though, prefer to classify multicellular algae as protoctists.

Two classes, mosses and liverworts, make up the bryophyte division. These plants lack the roots, stems, and leaves that are found in other plant divisions.

The fern group comprises four divisions of the plant kingdom: whisk ferns, club mosses, horsetails, and ferns. All members of the fern group have two stages in their life cycle. During one of these stages tiny reproductive structures, called spores, are released. These spores will eventually grow into a new plant.

More complex plants reproduce with seeds. Four divisions of plants reproduce with "naked" seeds in cones. Cycads, conifers, ginkgoes, and gnetophytes are all cone-bearing plants.

Two classes, monocots and dicots, make up the largest division of plants, the angiosperms, or flowering plants. Unlike cone-bearing plants, angiosperms reproduce with enclosed seeds such as berries, nuts, and fruits.

See Volume 17 for more information on the different divisions of plants.

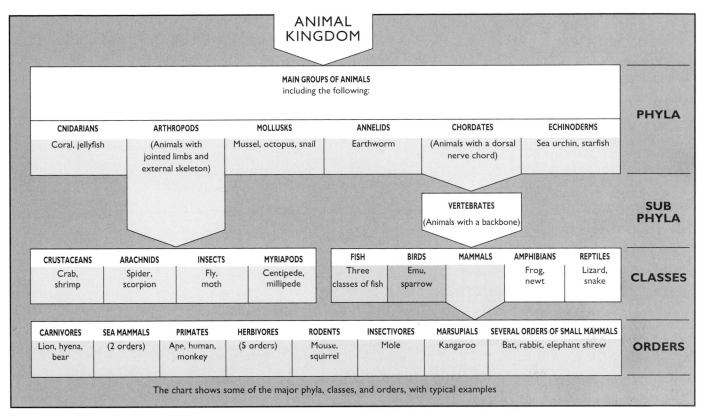

The chart shows some of the major phyla, classes, and orders, with typical examples

The chart content:

ANIMAL KINGDOM

MAIN GROUPS OF ANIMALS
including the following:

PHYLA

CNIDARIANS	ARTHROPODS	MOLLUSKS	ANNELIDS	CHORDATES	ECHINODERMS
Coral, jellyfish	(Animals with jointed limbs and external skeleton)	Mussel, octopus, snail	Earthworm	(Animals with a dorsal nerve chord)	Sea urchin, starfish

SUB PHYLA

VERTEBRATES
(Animals with a backbone)

CLASSES

CRUSTACEANS	ARACHNIDS	INSECTS	MYRIAPODS	FISH	BIRDS	MAMMALS	AMPHIBIANS	REPTILES
Crab, shrimp	Spider, scorpion	Fly, moth	Centipede, millipede	Three classes of fish	Emu, sparrow		Frog, newt	Lizard, snake

ORDERS

CARNIVORES	SEA MAMMALS	PRIMATES	HERBIVORES	RODENTS	INSECTIVORES	MARSUPIALS	SEVERAL ORDERS OF SMALL MAMMALS
Lion, hyena, bear	(2 orders)	Ape, human, monkey	(5 orders)	Mouse, squirrel	Mole	Kangaroo	Bat, rabbit, elephant shrew

The animal kingdom

In the eighteenth century, a botanist from Sweden named Carl von Linné (usually known by his Latin name, *Carolus Linneaus*) outlined a system of classifying plants and animals. This became the basis for classification all over the world. Scientists use Latin names so that all plants, animals, and other living things can be identified accurately, even though they have different common names in different places. Linneaus divided living organisms into two kingdoms: plants and animals. Today most scientists divide living things into five kingdoms: animals, plants, monerans, protoctists, and fungi. The animal kingdom (*above*) is divided into many phyla. Most of the phyla of the animal kingdom contain strange creatures — microscopic organisms, sponges, corals, slugs, and insects — without the backbone and central nervous system that we associate with more familiar animals.

Each phylum is divided into classes. For example, vertebrates (animals with a backbone) are a subdivision of a phylum and are divided up into seven classes: mammals, birds, reptiles, amphibians, and three classes of fish (represented by eels, sharks, and trout).

Each of these classes is broken down further into different orders. The mammal class, for instance, includes the orders carnivores (meat eaters), insectivores (insect eaters), primates (monkeys, apes), and marsupials (kangaroos, koalas), among others.

In this set of books, we give Latin names for different groups (genera) and kinds (species) of animals. See Volume 17 for more information on the different phyla of animals.

COLOR GUIDE

INVERTEBRATES

FISH

AMPHIBIANS & REPTILES

BIRDS

MAMMALS

PLANTS

BIOMES & HABITATS

MONERANS, PROTOCTISTS, & FUNGI

Butterfly

Butterflies (and moths) have one of the most dramatic life cycles of any member of the insect world. The cycle begins when the adult female butterfly lays her eggs, usually on the underside of a leaf that will be food for the growing caterpillar. These small, well-camouflaged eggs hatch out into long, fleshy caterpillars (a form of larva), which grow rapidly.

In spite of their length, caterpillars only have six true legs (as do all insects). These are attached to the top part of the body (the thorax), and the rest of the body is supported by stumps (not true legs), which in some cases are adapted to clasp stems. Down each side of the body is a row of holes (spiracles) through which the caterpillar breathes, as it has no lungs.

Caterpillars spend their time eating, feeding first on the casing of the egg and then on the leaves of the plant where they were laid. They sense their food with their antennae and the sensitive areas around their mouths.

Caterpillars grow rapidly and have to shed their skins several times to make room for this growth. Each time they shed their skin there is a new, elastic skin underneath, which gradually hardens as they develop.

Once the caterpillar has grown to a sufficient size, and when the season is right, it enters the next stage of its life cycle, changing from a caterpillar to a chrysalis or pupa. The caterpillar fixes its tail to a twig or leaf, using a silken thread that it spins itself. Some caterpillars wrap themselves in leaves, others spin a sling of silk, and others bury themselves underground. Once in position, the skin begins to split and is shed for the last time, revealing the shell of the chrysalis underneath. The shell starts to harden when it is exposed to the air.

A new look

The pupa or chrysalis appears to be completely dormant or inactive, but amazing changes are going on inside the case. The tissues that made up the

◀ *The wings of this brilliant Emerald swallowtail, like all butterfly wings, are made up of tiny scales.*

KEY FACTS

- **Name**
Swallowtail (*Papilio*, a subfamily of several hundred species)

- **Range**
Found in most parts of the world

- **Habitat**
Grasslands, swamps, marshes, scrubland, rainforest, and so on, according to species

- **Appearance**
Large, up to 5 in (12.5 cm) wingspan

- **Food**
Plant material

- **Breeding**
Large numbers of eggs, hatch into caterpillars and go through a pupal stage with no parental care

- **Status**
Some species are becoming rare; Homerus swallowtail (*Papilio homerus*) from Jamacia is endangered

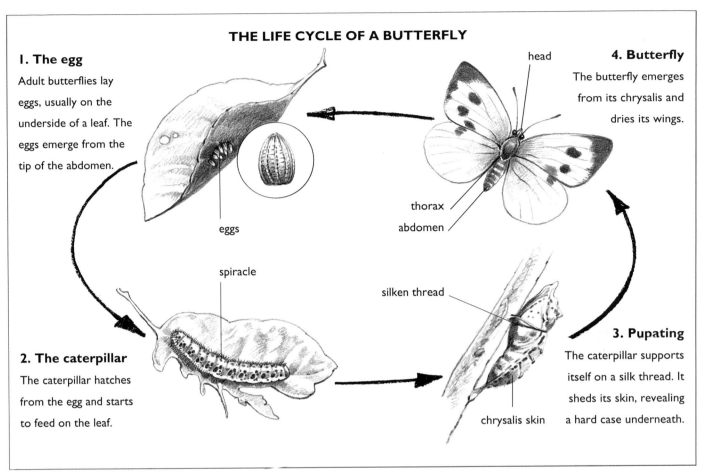

THE LIFE CYCLE OF A BUTTERFLY

1. The egg
Adult butterflies lay eggs, usually on the underside of a leaf. The eggs emerge from the tip of the abdomen.

eggs

spiracle

2. The caterpillar
The caterpillar hatches from the egg and starts to feed on the leaf.

head

4. Butterfly
The butterfly emerges from its chrysalis and dries its wings.

thorax
abdomen

silken thread

3. Pupating
The caterpillar supports itself on a silk thread. It sheds its skin, revealing a hard case underneath.

chrysalis skin

caterpillar are totally transformed into the parts of a butterfly. When the butterfly first emerges it has a fat abdomen (body) and limp wings. It rests in the sunshine until its wings are dry and it has pumped enough blood into the veins in the wings to hold them up stiffly.

The surface of the wings is made up of thousands of tiny overlapping scales. Butterflies have two pairs of wings, but the front and back wings are closely linked so that they operate as a single pair. The earliest known flying insects had two pairs of wings that operated independently.

One of the differences between a butterfly and a moth is the way they hold their wings when at rest: the butterfly holds its wings upright over its back, while the moth folds them flat so that they cover its abdomen.

Most butterflies feed on the nectar of particular flowers, although some eat fruit, sap from trees, or the sticky fluid made by aphids. They have a long, hollow feeding tube called a proboscis, which is a bit like a drinking straw, that they can uncoil to reach into flowers. Some have such a short adult life that they do not feed at all. Their eyes are compound eyes (large bulging eyes made up of lots of tubes) that give them good all-around vision.

Time scale
The length of each stage of the life cycle depends on the type of butterfly and where it lives. In some species, it only

▲ *The butterfly first hatches from its egg as a caterpillar, and then pupates before emerging as a butterfly. This is known as a complete metamorphosis.*

KEY FACTS

● **Name**
Monarch
(*Danaus plexippus*)

● **Range**
Most of North
America, migrating
south to Mexico in
winter

● **Habitat**
Butterfly flowers
(*Asclepias* species);
eucalyptus and pine
trees during winter

● **Appearance**
Golden brown wings
with dark veins and
white spots around
the edges

● **Food**
Plants on which they
lay eggs

● **Breeding**
Mate and lay eggs as
they migrate north;
they go through
larval and pupal
stages, then emerge
as adults that
continue to migrate

● **Status**
Widespread

▶ *Monarch butterflies migrate to one place in Mexico. The whole species spends the winter here, so they are vulnerable to predators.*

takes a few weeks from the time the eggs are laid until the time the butterfly is fully developed. A typical pattern is that the parent lays eggs in the fall, and they hatch into caterpillars in spring. These form chrysalises in early summer and develop into butterflies within a couple of weeks. However, in many species they spend the winter in the chrysalis or butterfly form as well. Neither the egg nor the chrysalis will hatch unless the conditions are right.

Some butterflies migrate annually, heading toward the equator during the winter months, and flying back to cooler zones to lay their eggs. The Monarch butterfly, for example, gathers in small groups in the fall all over North America and heads south. Gradually, small groups meet up together until, when they reach the warmer climate of Mexico, there are millions in a single swarm.

They spread themselves over trees and rest (rather like hibernating mammals) until the weather is warm enough to head north again. They lay eggs on their way north, and the new generation of butterflies continues the northward migration during the summer months. Marked butterflies have been observed to travel over 1500 miles (2400 km).

Defense mechanisms

The caterpillar and chrysalis stages are particularly vulnerable to predators. These insects have found many different ways of protecting themselves. Most caterpillars feed on the underside of leaves, where they are hidden from their main enemies – birds. Many caterpillars are colored to blend with their surroundings, which usually means they are green. Their shape may add to the camouflage effect – long thin caterpillars blend with the ribs on the backs of leaves. Some caterpillars eat poisonous plants, such as deadly nightshade, which gives them a bitter flavor to put off their enemies, while others have bright red and black or yellow

NATURAL HABITAT

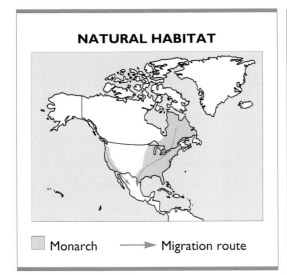

Monarch ⟶ Migration route

and black stripes to act as a warning to birds. For example, the caterpillar of a swallowtail butterfly has strong red and black markings on its fat green body. It also produces acid from a gland in its neck. Once a predator has tasted the caterpillar it will be sure to avoid caterpillars with similar markings. Some other species take advantage of this fact and have developed markings that mimic poisonous or distasteful species.

At the pupal stage, most species imitate twigs or dried leaves. They are almost motionless, which makes them less easy to see than the caterpillar. Some species actually adapt the coloring of their outer case to blend with their surroundings, so that if they are surrounded by dead leaves or bark they are brown, but if they are in lush foliage they are green.

Color in adults

The sole purpose in life of the adult butterfly (known as the imago) is to reproduce and ensure that the eggs are laid in a place where they are likely to survive. While some species are carefully

▼ *The markings of this Buckeye butterfly from Florida make it look as if there are huge eyes on its wings. This fools their predators (mainly birds) into thinking that they are looking at a small mammal rather than a tasty butterfly. The same sort of patterning is found on many different species of butterfly.*

disguised to blend with their surroundings, often imitating leaves or bark, others are brightly colored to attract suitable mates. In some cases the female has more subdued markings than the male.

Butterflies usually perch on plants with their wings back to back and the undersides, which show in this position, are a softer color than the bright uppersides of some species.

In some species the coloring acts as a warning to predators. Eye markings on wings startle enemies, while some strong markings warn that they are distasteful. Like the caterpillars, some butterflies mimic the markings of a distasteful butterfly as a form of defense.

The adults have special scales on their wings that give off a scent called a pheromone to attract the opposite sex. The adults have their sexual organs in their tails and, after mating, the female flies off to find a suitable plant on which to lay her eggs. The number laid varies immensely between species — some African butterflies have been found to lay 350 at a time.

Cactus

Cacti are flowering plants native to the semideserts of the Americas. There are over 1400 species in this family (*Cactaceae*), which come in a huge variety of shapes and sizes. The smallest cactus in the world is *Blossfeldia liliputana* from South America with a diameter of just ¼ in (5 mm). The largest is the branching Saguaro cactus (*Carnegiea gigantea*) of the southwestern U.S. and Mexico, which may reach 60 ft (18 m) in height and weigh more than 10 tons (9 tonnes).

Adaptations to drought

Cacti may be herbs, climbing vines, shrubs, or trees. All are extremely well adapted to an arid, or dry, environment. Cacti belong to a large group of plants known as succulents, which comes from the Latin word *succulentis,* meaning "juicy." This name describes the swollen, fleshy stems of these plants, which are excellent storage organs. The 10-ft- (3-m-) tall *Echinocactus ingens* can hold up to 210 gallons (800 liters) of water (enough to sustain the plant for several years during a drought). In many species, the stem has ribs or pleats like an accordion. These ribs allow the stem to swell with water during wet periods or contract into a thin, shriveled trunk during dry periods. The whole plant also has a thick, waxy

▲ *A giant Saguaro cactus is a common sight in the semideserts of the southwestern U.S. and Mexico. This plant has a number of adaptations to the dry, parched environment in which it is found. Its fleshy stem can hold hundreds of gallons of water, which is essential if the plant is to survive several years of drought.*

covering known as a cuticle, which also helps the plant to retain water.

Another adaptation of the cactus is its root system. In the creeping, vine-type cactus known as Queen-of-the-night (*Peniocereus greggi*), which is found hanging from other trees in tropical rainforests, a single huge root may weigh as much as 75 lb (35 kg).

Most cacti do not have leaves, so the stem takes on the role of photosynthesis, the process of producing food from light and carbon dioxide (CO_2). Exceptions to this rule are the thorn shrub species in the genus *Pereskia*. *Pereskia* spp. have large leaves and thin stems. In other cacti, the leaves are modified into sharp spines and fine hairs, which are held on tiny structures called areoles all over the plant.

The spines help protect the plant in a number of ways: they catch and take in tiny drops of dew and moist air, which help prevent the plant from drying out; they reflect sunlight and shade the stem during times of intense sun, or insulate it when it is cold; and they defend the cactus from browsing animals. In some species, there is a tuft of even sharper bristles on the areoles, known as glochids. These have hooked barbs that puncture an animal's skin, often causing painful swellings.

NATURAL HABITAT

☐ Saguaro cactus

Brilliant flowers and juicy fruit

Many cacti have attractive flowers, often in blazing reds, yellows, and blues. These brightly colored flowers attract a number of pollinators. Bees are a particular favorite, pollinating up to 90 percent of all cacti species. Some cacti have brilliant white, strongly scented flowers, which open only at night and are pollinated by nocturnal moths and bats. For example, the Saguaro cactus is regularly pollinated by Lesser long-nosed bats (*Leptonycteris curasoae*) on their yearly migration between Mexico and the southwestern U.S.

The seeds of cacti are contained in fleshy berries, which are often red, white, or lilac in color. Many cacti berries are edible and eaten not only by birds and other animals, such as goats and deer, but also by humans. One such tasty fruit is the prickly pear from the genus *Opuntia*.

Humans have also used cacti for many other items, such as wood for fence palings and emergency supplies of moist food when traveling through dry, parched deserts. The cacti have also long been ornamental house plants.

Out of control

Spurges (*Euphorbia* spp.) in Africa, Europe, Asia, and Australia are often mistaken for cacti, but the two groups of plants are completely unrelated. However, although cacti originated in the Americas, various species have also been introduced by humans or birds and other animals into different parts of the world, such as the Mediterranean, Africa, and Australia. Sometimes this has had unfortunate consequences. For example, during the nineteenth century, one species of prickly pear, *Opuntia stricta,* was imported into Australia. Grazing animals could not feed on these cacti, and optimum conditions meant that prickly pears soon multiplied and became weeds. Within just 75 years, it had covered an area of 60 million acres (24 million hectares). Eventually, the cactus was brought back under control when a predatory moth caterpillar known as *Cactoblastis* was introduced from Argentina in 1925.

Today, the ornamental value of many cacti has led to their overcollection in the wild. To protect these endangered plants, many countries banned the trade in wild cacti.

KEY FACTS

● **Name**
Saguaro cactus
(*Carnegiea gigantea*)

● **Range**
Southwestern U.S. and northwestern Mexico

● **Habitat**
Desert regions

● **Appearance**
A tall, tree-like cactus, growing up to 60 ft (18 m) high and weighing up to 10 tons (9 tonnes); a green, column-like stem and large, upward-branching arms covered in numerous spine-bearing areoles; white flowers; edible fruit

● **Life cycle**
Perennial

● **Uses**
Food (fruit, seeds, wine); ornamental

● **Status**
Common within its range

◄ *Many cacti have brightly colored flowers. The golden-yellow flowers of this prickly pear (Opuntia sp.) are designed to attract pollinating insects such as moths and bees.*

Caddis fly

Caddis flies are small, winged insects that are closely related to butterflies and moths. However, unlike some species of brightly colored moths and butterflies, adult caddis flies are a rather drab brownish color. Caddis flies are better known for the fascinating cases constructed by the caddis "worm" or larva.

A changing life

Caddis flies are advanced insects that undergo what is known as complete metamorphosis. This means that their life cycle involves several different changes in body shape, from egg through larva, pupa, and adult.

Once a year in the fall, the male adult caddis flies, with their keen eyesight and long antennae, find the females and try to attract them by sending out pheromones (special chemical scents) and flying or

▲ *Some species of adult caddis flies swarm during the day, but most are active at night and spend the day resting in cool, dark places.*

dancing in huge vertical swarms. The males and females then mate while they are flying. The female lays a mass of tiny round eggs — each of them measuring about a tenth of an inch (0.3 mm) — that are white or pale blue-green in color. These are covered in a sticky substance, so that the female can attach them to plants or stones close to fresh water in small streams or ponds.

Building a beautiful case

When the eggs hatch, small, caterpillar-like larvae emerge and drop into the water. For camouflage and protection from predators such as fish, many species of caddis larva construct a beautiful

KEY FACTS

● **Name**
Large caddis fly (family name, *Phryganeidae*)

● **Range**
Worldwide

● **Habitat**
Near streams, ponds, small lakes

● **Appearance**
Adults have elongated bodies, measuring $1/20$-$1 1/2$ in (1.5-35 mm), with 4 hairy wings, long, thread-like antennae and compound eyes; larvae are caterpillar-like with 3 pairs of legs, a patch of simple eyes on each side of the head; small antennae and chewing mouthparts

● **Food**
Underwater vegetation, plankton, small crustaceans

● **Breeding**
Females lay a mass of eggs once a year that hatch into larvae during the winter, pupate in spring and emerge as adults in early summer

● **Status**
Widespread

portable case or shell made of spun silk and decorated with pieces of vegetation, sand, or small stones. This case is stuck to the larva's skin. Some species, on the other hand, do not construct these cases, but instead make small silken nets attached to plants and stones. These nets face upstream and catch food for the larvae — mainly small crustaceans (water animals with shells) and plankton (tiny plants and animals) — as it floats down the stream.

The larvae spend the winter feeding and growing, shedding their skin and their shells several times and constructing new ones. Eventually, in spring, they use the shell as a covering when they pupate.

Inside the shell, the body is completely transformed, and an adult caddis fly emerges in the early summer, cutting its way out of the pupa case with powerful mandibles (jaws). It then climbs up a piece of vegetation to reach the surface of the water and flies off into the air.

Adult caddis flies

Adult caddis flies have elongated bodies that are about ¾ in (20 mm) long. They have two sets of hairy, transparent wings — the forewings are generally slightly larger than the hind wings — and long, thread-like antennae. Like many insects, they have compound eyes made up of hundreds of tiny lenses or facets, which are very sensitive to light. Although its mouthparts are able to lick up liquid, the adult caddis fly has rarely been seen to feed and some species do not feed at all.

Thousands of species

There are about 5000 species of caddis fly found throughout the world, including large caddis flies (*Phryganeidae*), micro caddis flies (*Hydroptilidae*), and primitive caddis flies (*Limnephilidae*). Most species are found near fresh water, although an Australian species called *Philanisus plebeius* breeds in rock pools by the sea.

◄ *Caddis fly larvae are omnivorous and use their chewing mouthparts to feed on underwater plants and creatures called plankton that are too small to see. They have a tiny pair of false legs on the tip of the abdomen, which hold the larva inside its magnificent case, and three pairs of legs attached to the main part of the body.*

See also Butterfly, Dragonfly, Fly, Moth

Camel

KEY FACTS

- **Name**
  Bactrian camel
  (*Camelus bactrianus*)

- **Range**
  Mongolia, China

- **Habitat**
  Desert, semi-desert,
  steppe grassland,
  mountainous regions

- **Appearance**
  A large body,
  measuring as much
  as 10 ft (3 m) with a
  tail of 22 in (55 cm);
  two humps; short,
  light brown coat in
  summer, with a long
  and woolly winter
  coat; a mane and
  beard-like hair on
  the throat

- **Food**
  Grasses and foliage

- **Breeding**
  1 calf (rarely 2), is
  active within 48
  hours and is suckled
  for 9-18 months

- **Status**
  Endangered

Camels are strong and hardy animals. They are perfectly adapted for life in dry, desert regions and have been extremely valuable in helping man to travel and survive in these bleak areas of the world. There are two main types of camel: the Bactrian camel (two-humped) and the dromedary (one-humped).

Surviving in the desert

There are many features of the camel that make it well suited to desert life. It can tolerate large variations in its body temperature, which prevents it from perspiring and losing the moisture that is essential for its survival in the desert. It is able to conserve water very efficiently and can go for long periods without drinking. Indeed, the camel is able to withstand losing 25 percent of its body weight in water without any ill effects (compared with humans who cannot lose more than three or four percent!).

Like other mammals, the camel stores energy in its body. However, most mammals store this energy in the form of a layer of fat that covers the whole body, which helps to keep the animal warm. The camel, on the other hand, needs to be able to lose heat quickly, and so it stores most of its fat in one place — in the hump (or humps) on its back. This fat store is a valuable source of energy, which the camel can use when it is forced to feed on the poorest of desert vegetation.

Chewing the cud

Like the cow, the camel is a ruminant. This means that it has a complicated digestive system. It eats any kind of tough, desert foliage that it can find, chewing and swallowing it. The camel then brings its food back up to its mouth in order to chew it for a second time. This is called chewing the cud, and it allows the camel to get as much valuable nutrition from the food as possible. Camels usually spend the morning searching for food and chew the cud in the afternoon.

Unlike other hoofed mammals, only the front of the camel's hoofs touch the ground. It rests its body load on large, flexible foot pads that expand and prevent the camel from sinking into the soft sand.

Camels also have long, thick eyelashes arranged in double rows and nostrils that can be closed. These protect the eyes and nose from windblown sand and dust in harsh sandstorms, and they also help to cut down on loss of moisture.

Young calves

During the calving season — usually once every two years — the females give birth in a standing position, producing one (or more rarely, two) calf. As soon as they are born, the young calves are like miniature versions of their parents. They can begin to walk unsteadily after two or three hours and are fully active after 48 hours. They are suckled for a year on milk that is extremely watery — the calf gets much of its essential water from its mother in these early stages of its life — and are able to feed on vegetation within two months. Female calves become fully mature in three to four years and males in about six years.

▼ *In the wild, female Bactrian camels live in herds and only meet up with males at mating time. Males, on the other hand, form small bachelor groups or become solitary animals wandering the desert alone.*

◀ *Dromedaries look very different from Bactrian camels. They have only one hump, and much shorter, coarser hair. Their legs are also longer, and they develop hard, worn patches or callosities on their leg joints and chests where they touch the ground when they are sitting down.*

The Bactrian camel

The Bactrian camel has a very distinctive appearance. Unlike the dromedary, which only has one hump, the Bactrian camel has two humps on its back where it stores fat. During the winter it has a long, dark brown coat, which is very thick and shaggy, protecting it from the harsh weather. It sheds this warm coat during the summer, leaving a short, light brown covering with thin manes on its chin, shoulders, hind legs, and humps.

Bactrian camels are extremely peaceful. They move very slowly, ambling along with a kind of rolling walk — lifting up both legs on one side at the same time. They also have relatively short legs (especially compared with those of the dromedary) that enable them to walk easily on hilly and rocky ground.

The Bactrian camel is named after part of the region where it once lived — Baktria, on the border between Turkestan and Afghanistan. It was first tamed and used by humans in about the third century B.C., when wild Bactrian camels were still widespread throughout their range.

Today the wild Bactrian camel is endangered and there are no more than 500 left, confined to the Gobi desert, which is on the Chinese-Mongolian border. However, domestic Bactrian camels can be found in Afghanistan, Turkey, Iran, and China.

The dromedary

The dromedary is also known as the Arabian camel, and was originally

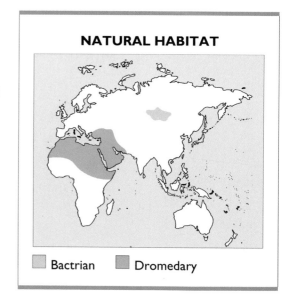

NATURAL HABITAT

☐ Bactrian   ☐ Dromedary

found in hot, desert regions in North Africa, Arabia, and the Middle East. Dromedaries have very short, coarse hair that is particularly thick on the upper surfaces of its body – the top of its head, neck, and hump. This gives the camel effective protection from the hot desert sun. The rest of its body is almost naked, allowing any excess heat to escape.

Another interesting feature of the dromedary is the fact that its body temperature drops at night and rises slowly during the day, so that the camel does not need to sweat for long to keep cool. This prevents it from losing water.

There are actually two types of dromedary. One of them is very heavily built and moves slowly. This is mainly used by humans as a beast of burden, carrying heavy loads across the desert. The other is much lighter and a graceful runner, often used for riding.

There have been no truly wild dromedaries in existence for the last 2000 years. However, there are many controlled or domesticated camels, and feral dromedaries (tame camels that have been released into the wild) live in many parts of the world, including Australia.

The camelids

As well as the dromedary and the Bactrian camel, the camel family also includes a group of smaller animals that are known as camelids. These animals are all found in South America, where the guanaco and the vicuna occur in the wild, and the llama and alpaca are domesticated.

KEY FACTS

- **Name**
  Dromedary
  (*Camelus dromedarius*)

- **Range**
  North Africa, Arabia,
  Middle East

- **Habitat**
  Desert

- **Appearance**
  A single hump; beige
  or light brown coat
  with a slightly lighter
  underside; head and
  body up to 10 ft
  (3 m) long, with a tail
  of 22 in (55 cm)

- **Food**
  Any kind of grasses
  and foliage

- **Breeding**
  1 calf born after a
  gestation period of
  about 13 months

- **Status**
  In captivity and feral

◄ *Dromedaries were first tamed by tribespeople around 300 B.C. in Arabia. As well as carrying heavy loads and being used for riding, these useful camels provided meat, milk, wool, and manure.*

See also **Llama**

Capybara

The capybara is the largest living rodent in the world. Also known as the Orinoco hog, it is about the size of a domestic pig and may grow to over 3 ft (1 m) in length. The capybara is only found in South America, living in a variety of different habitats – from tropical forests to open grasslands – wherever there is water.

Efficient swimmers

Capybaras are herbivores and graze on water plants, or grasses and vegetation on the banks of rivers, lakes, and swamps. They mainly graze in the late afternoon and evening, spending the morning resting, and bathing when the sun is at its hottest in the middle of the day.

Capybaras are well adapted to life in the water. They have webbed feet that help them to swim well, and small eyes, ears, and nostrils located on top of their heads so that they can be held above the water level easily.

Even mating takes place in the water. This may be at any time during the year and, after five months, a litter of about four young are born. Their mother goes back to the group after a couple of hours. The young join her and the rest of the group after three or four days, and – along with other babies from different mothers – are watched over by several nursing females.

While resting and feeding, capybaras are always on the alert for predators – foxes, jaguars, and vultures – that prey on the vulnerable infants. If one of the capybaras detects a predator approaching, it gives an "alarm" bark or makes a coughing sound, which causes the rest of the group to stop what they are doing and stand alert. If the predator stays in the area, the alarm call is repeated over and over again and the capybaras rush into the water, forming a tight group with the young in the center, as far away from danger as possible. These

◀ *Capybaras are very good swimmers and can dive below the surface for up to five minutes at a time.*

▶ *Young capybaras are well developed at birth. They are fully mobile after two or three days, and can eat grass within a week. They are extremely vocal and constantly make a purring noise when they are active.*

tactics are particularly effective when they are faced with one of their most feared predators – the alligator-like cayman.

NATURAL HABITAT

☐ Capybara

Strong teeth

Like many other rodents, capybaras have angular skulls and very well-developed front teeth (called incisors) for cropping vegetation. These keep on growing throughout the capybara's life, in order to make up for the constant wear and tear that is caused by such heavy grazing.

Male and female capybaras generally look alike, although the large scent gland located on top of their snouts – known as the morrillo – is much easier to see in dominant males. Small "family" groups are often made up of one dominant male with several females and their young, and one or more younger males. However, many of these small groups gather around water pools during the dry season and may form much larger groups of 50-60 animals.

Capybara farming

In the past, capybaras have been widely hunted by humans for meat and hides, and their fat was used in medicine. Today in Venzuela, they are even farmed for these products. Much of their natural habitat has also been drained for use as cattle pasture.

However, despite a drastic decline in their numbers, capybaras are still extremely widespread and are found in many National Parks and reserves throughout South America.

See also **Coypu**

Cardinal

the last 50 years their range has extended northwards, mainly because people have gotten into the habit of putting out birdseed and tidbits in their gardens during the winter. Some lesser-known, related species are only found in rainforests.

Living on the edge

In the wild, the cardinal lives on the fringe of forest or woodland where it is sheltered by trees and undergrowth but can easily venture out to feed. Its favorite food is seeds, and it has a tough, conical beak and strong muscles so that it can crack open hard seed cases. Birds with beaks like this are often known as grosbeaks or buntings. In the summer, the Northern cardinal will feed on insects and fruit, but come the fall and through the winter it usually relies on seeds – or whatever is in the nearest birdfeeder.

The bright color of the male (bright red, with reddish-brown wings and a distinctive black face around a red beak) is a warning

A red male cardinal is a startling sight against the snow in a New England garden. You might think that such a colorful bird would be more at home in a tropical jungle, and this is not far from the truth. Known as Northern cardinals, these friendly birds used to be found only in the southern states of America, but in

▲ *A male cardinal, in handsome plumage, sings out a clear "Cheear, cheear, cheear; whoit, whoit, whoit" to mark out his home ground.*

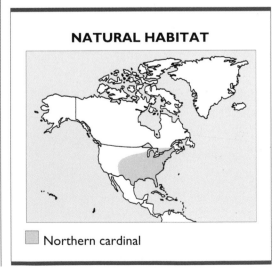

NATURAL HABITAT

Northern cardinal

◄ The female cardinal, a pretty fawn color, has the same crest and wedge-shaped beak as the male. The beak is very strong, for eating seeds and grains.

KEY FACTS

● **Name**
Northern cardinal
(*Cardinalis cardinalis*)

● **Range**
South and eastern U.S., Arizona to Florida, and north to New England and Canada

● **Habitat**
Woodlands and suburban gardens

● **Appearance**
8$^{1}/_{2}$-9 in (22-23 cm); male has bright red feathers on his head, breast, and tail, touches of brown on wings; high red crest; red wedge-shaped beak and black face

● **Food**
Seeds, grains, fruit, and insects

● **Breeding**
Nests low down, in shrubs and hedges; 3-4 eggs

● **Status**
Widespread

to other birds not to come near his territory. He chases away other males. In spring as the weather gets milder, he sings a cheerful tune of repeated whistling sounds with several different tones, to attract a mate and tell competitors that he is setting up home here. The female helps to stake out the territory with a similar song to her mate. She, however, has much more subtle coloring: a pinkish-buff back with touches of red on wings, crest, and tail, and a paler breast and underparts.

Working together

Pairs of birds work together to build a rather untidy, loose nest. They usually choose low bushes, hedges, or small trees and find the shelter of a suburban garden ideal. The nest is lined with soft feathers, hairs, and grasses.

The female lays three or four eggs, which are off-white with purplish-brown markings. The eggs take a couple of weeks to hatch, and during this time the female (partly disguised by her soft coloring) sits on them while the male collects food for her. When the eggs hatch, both parents have a busy time collecting food. Sometimes, a second female (probably a one-year-old from the previous year's brood) helps with the feeding of the young. Each pair may produce two or three broods a year.

Through the summer months, when food is plentiful, the main enemy of these birds is the domestic cat. Cats stalk the flower beds on the lookout for young fledglings who do not have the experience to know when to stop foraging and take flight. If you are putting out food for these cheerful little birds in winter, always hang it from a branch or use a bird feeder that is well out of the reach of any cats prowling the neighborhood.

Caribou

◄ *Unlike other species of deer, both male and female caribou have antlers. However, those of the males are heavier and much more complex, sometimes growing up to 3 ft (1 m) in length. The dominant male uses his massive antlers to impress the females and threaten other males, and he displays them proudly by walking alongside a rival to show their size.*

The caribou is a large deer that lives in the arctic tundra of Alaska, Canada, Asia, and Scandinavia. It is a robust animal, with a thick, waterproof coat to protect it from the harsh winter weather. Its legs are long, with broad hoofs that expand as it walks, preventing it from sinking into the snow. Huge, impressive antlers, with many complicated branches, enable the caribou to scrape away the deep, frozen snow to graze on the vegetation buried beneath, and are useful weapons when it is defending grazing rights on such thinly vegetated land.

There is a yearly cycle in which the caribou's antlers keep growing larger and larger until they are full size. Then they are shed, ready for the new ones to grow. When the antlers are growing, they are made of living tissue, with a blood supply and a covering of skin known as velvet. This velvet peels off once the antlers have grown to full size, revealing a hard, bony material. After a few months, these antlers are shed and new ones start to grow. The peeling of the velvet is very

NATURAL HABITAT

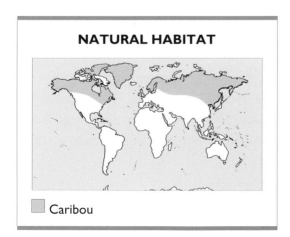

☐ Caribou

KEY FACTS

● **Name**
Caribou
(*Rangifer tarandus*)

● **Range**
Canada, Alaska,
Eurasia

● **Habitat**
Arctic tundra,
coniferous forests

● **Appearance**
Large body,
measuring 3½-7 ft
(1.2-2.2 m), with
a tail of 3-8 in
(7-20 cm); a thick
coat, which varies in
color, but is mostly
brownish above and
paler below; both
sexes carry large
antlers – up to 3 ft
(1 m) long in males

● **Food**
Lichens, leaves,
berries, twigs,
shoots, fungi, grasses

● **Breeding**
1 (rarely 2) calves,
which can keep up
with the herd within
1 day of birth

● **Status**
Common in some
areas; some
subspecies are
endangered

▶ *A herd of caribou
run from one of their
greatest predators –
the wolf.*

irritating to the caribou, and it constantly rubs its antlers against trees and bushes to remove it in time for the mating season.

Migrating in huge herds

During the summer, female caribou form small herds with their young and feed on lichens and other vegetation in the northernmost part of their home range. Dominant males are solitary and wander from herd to herd mating with suitable females, while younger males form small groups of their own.

Although some woodland caribou remain in the same place all year round, others migrate. During the winter, they travel south to find food and shelter from the harsh arctic weather. All the groups join together to form one huge herd – often numbering up to 100,000 individuals. Then they start the long trek south following traditional routes for as far as 800 miles (1300 km). Older and more experienced animals lead the way as the caribou trudge in long columns, searching for shelter from the driving wind and snow. There is safety in numbers, as predators such as wolves only tackle individual animals, and traveling in a large herd makes the chances of being preyed upon much lower.

The caribou only stop when they reach the protection of a forest, where they will stay for the rest of the winter. They strip the bark from the trees, eat the moss and lichens that grow on them, and use their hoofs and antlers to clear away patches of snow so that they can feed on ground vegetation. Then, in the spring when the snow has melted, the caribou start the long journey back to their breeding grounds in the north.

Reindeer

The European caribou (known as the reindeer) has been brought under control by the Lapps, who travel with the herds as they migrate across northern Norway.

See also Deer, Elk, Moose

Carp

The common carp originally lived in the rivers that emptied into the Black Sea and the Aegean Sea in Eastern Europe. Carp fishbones have been found in prehistoric sites in that area, which proves that they have been caught for food for thousands of years. Because carp are such a useful source of food, humans have introduced them into most other parts of the world, although more recently carp have been used to stock rivers and lakes for sportsmen to catch, rather than as a major food source.

A quiet lifestyle

The carp is not a particularly fast or strong swimmer and lives in quiet

▲ *The common carp lives in slow-moving rivers, lakes, and ponds. Carp can grow to quite a size and have been known to live for as long as 20 years in the wild – and even longer if they are in captivity.*

backwaters, lakes, and pools rather than fast-flowing streams. Carp pick around through weeds and on the bottom, feeding on small crustaceans (shrimp-like creatures) and the young of thousands of different insects, which are found in fresh water. They also eat plant matter, and some adults eat mollusks and small fish.

Breathing and breeding

Carp can tolerate much warmer water than some fish. The higher the water temperature, the less oxygen can dissolve in it. For this reason, many fish prefer cooler water, but the carp's gills are able to cope with the lower quantity of oxygen in warmer habitats.

Carp have been introduced to cooler habitats (in the northern part of North America and Britain). However, they have not bred as successfully in these areas as in their natural habitat.

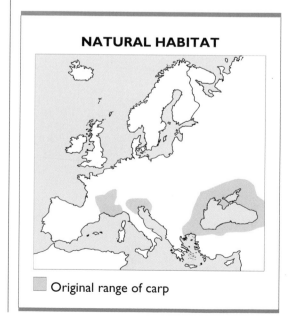

NATURAL HABITAT

Original range of carp

KEY FACTS

- **Name**
  Carp (*Cyprinus carpio*)

- **Range**
  Originally European, but has been introduced to most parts of the world

- **Habitat**
  Ponds, lakes, and slow-flowing rivers

- **Appearance**
  Deep-bodied, silvery fish, up to 40 in (1 m) long, with an upright back fin; large mouth

- **Food**
  Small crustaceans, insect larvae; some plants

- **Breeding**
  Need warm conditions 74-77°F (23-25°C)

- **Status**
  Widespread

▶ *These domesticated carp have been specially bred for their bright and interesting colors. Goldfish and Koi carp are carp-shaped fish, related to the common carp.*

Most carp will only breed when the water temperature reaches 74-77°F (23-25°C) in the summer months. A pair of carp often perform a courtship ritual, splashing and rolling in quite shallow water before the female lays her eggs. The male then deposits his sperm over the eggs. Like most fish, the adults leave the eggs to hatch and the young fish to develop without any parental care. However, the eggs do get some protection from pond and river weed.

In order to ensure that a sufficient number of young grow into adults to keep the species going, the female lays hundreds of eggs. The young are at risk from larger species of fish and birds such as the kingfisher, but the vast numbers ensure that some survive into adulthood. Carp are long-lived fish and have been known to survive for 20 years in the wild.

In common with most fish, carp have a covering of mucus, which gives them their wet, slimy feel. This helps them to glide through the water, and protects them against parasites that may invade them. (Just as we can get fungal infections such as athlete's foot or ringworm, carp and other fish are prone to their own fungi.)

Farming methods

Carp are now farmed in parts of eastern Europe and in Israel where the climate is warm enough. In captivity, two interesting varieties have been produced through selective breeding: the mirror carp, which only has a couple of rows of large scales down either side of its body (looking like a line of mirrors), and the leather carp, which has no scales at all.

In the wild, a fish's scales help to protect it by acting as camouflage: the transparent scales allow the silvery color of the skin to show through; and they reflect light, like a mirror. Once in captivity, however, they no longer need their camouflage.

Catfish

◀ *Bullheads have particularly fine whiskers, or barbels, and use them to feel for prey in the dark waters where they live. Their color helps to camouflage them in the mud.*

The name "catfish" is used to describe a whole range of different species of fish that have one thing in common — long whiskers or barbels that they use to feel their way along the bottom. Typical catfish have long bodies and flattened heads with wide mouths for scooping up their food. This large variety of fish has an equally large variety of habitats, from the Amazon basin to the rivers of Europe and from the Mississippi delta to the Mekong estuary.

Some are prized as aquarium specimens, some are caught by anglers for food or sport, some are fascinating to scientists, and others are of very little interest at all!

North American catfish

One or two types of catfish are saltwater fish, but most dwell in fresh water. There are several well-known species of freshwater catfish in North America. The Channel catfish is widespread, from southern Canada to Mexico and Florida. The Blue catfish or Mississippi cat has a more restricted range. Both the Channel and Blue catfish grow to a large size and make a tasty meal. The adult Blue catfish may be 5 ft (1.5 m) long, and weights of up to 80 lb (36 kg) are often recorded. Flatheads are longer and thinner than most catfish, and are found from the

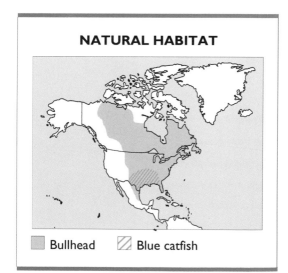

NATURAL HABITAT

[legend] Bullhead   Blue catfish

rivers running north into the Great Lakes down to Arkansas, Oklahoma, and Mexico.

Down on the bottom

Catfish are bottom-living fish, lurking under stones and vegetation, eating invertebrates and small fish. Many species of catfish build nests for their young and some, like the Brown bullhead (a close relative of the Blue catfish), not only tend the eggs in shallow hollows scooped in the mud, but they also protect the newly hatched young and attack intruders.

Adult North American catfish have few enemies because they are so large. However, they are well camouflaged, with dark coloring on their backs as a disguise when they are lurking on the bottom. Their undersides are much paler, so that if they do rise to the surface any predators lurking below will have difficulty seeing them — the silvery coloring blends with the silvery surface of the river or lake.

One South American catfish has a mottled underside to blend in with dappled sunlight on the surface of the water.

Clever cousins

There is a large number of tropical species of catfish, many of which are scaleless or have bony plates down either side to protect them. There are also marine catfish, such as the Sea catfish (*Arius felis*). This species, which lives mainly in sandy-bottomed harbors and estuaries eating crabs, shrimp, and small fish, is particularly interesting because of its breeding technique. When the female lays her eggs, she holds them in a flap beneath one of her pairs of fins until the male has mated with her. The male then takes the eggs into his mouth and holds them there until they have hatched — and for a couple of weeks after. For this reason, the male cannot eat anything for about six weeks during the summer.

KEY FACTS

- **Name**
  Brown bullhead
  (*Ictalurus nebulosus*)

- **Range**
  Eastern North America, from southern Canada to Florida and Atlanta; now introduced to western U.S., New Zealand, and Europe

- **Habitat**
  Bottom of freshwater rivers and lakes

- **Appearance**
  18 in (46 cm); dark yellow-brown back, blotched sides, greenish-yellow underside; barbels

- **Food**
  Invertebrates

- **Breeding**
  Spawn in nests, the parents care for the young

- **Status**
  Widespread

◄ *This Walking catfish (Clarias batrachus) from Malaysia lives in dark places such as caves. It can manage well in water with little oxygen. In fact, it can survive out of water and "walks" out in search of food.*

155

Cattail

Cattails are familiar reed-like aquatic plants. They are often found growing around the edges of open fresh or salty water, in lakes, marshes, and ponds; in both temperate and cold regions; and in the northern and southern hemisphere. Cattails are members of a small family, called the *Typhaceae*, made up of around 12 different species. They are all wetland herbs, which tend to grow together in large clusters or colonies. They are closely related to plants in the bur reed family (*Sparganiaceae*). The Common cattail (*Typha latifolia*) and the Narrow-leaved cattail (*Typha angustifolia*) are two species that occur in North America.

Cat's tail

The Common cattail is a tall plant, sometimes reaching a height of 8 ft (2.5 m) or more, with long, flat, grass-like leaves measuring from ⅓-⅗ in (around 8-15 mm) across. As its name suggests, the Narrow-leaved cattail has much narrower leaves, which grow to only half the width of those of its cousin. The base of the stems and leaves are usually beneath the surface of the water in both species.

▲ *The Common cattail is common to the wetlands of Eurasia and North America. The plant got its name for the dark brown, furry inflorescence that grows on top of the stem, which looks rather like the tail of a cat. The inflorescence is made up of numerous tiny flowers.*

One of the most recognizable features of cattails is the dark brown, furry, sausage-shaped structure that develops toward the top of the thick stem, making the plant look somewhat like the upright tail of a cat. This is actually made up of numerous tiny female flowers, and it is topped by a thinner, fluffy spike of lighter brown or yellow male flowers. This kind of spike made up of many flowers is known as an inflorescence.

In the Common cattail, the flower spikes are relatively fat, and the male flowers usually grow directly atop the female flowers. In the Narrow-leaved cattail, the two much thinner spikes are distinct and separated by a short piece of stem. Like grasses, cattails are pollinated by the wind, so they do not expend energy producing bright, colorful flowers with strong scents and nectar to attract insects or other animal pollinators. The fruits are also dispersed by the wind, and they have a tiny stalk covered with light hairs to help them float on the air currents.

Cattails are very competitive plants, and they spread rapidly, crowding out other plants aggressively. Sometimes they can

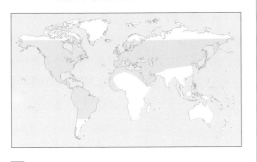

NATURAL HABITAT

☐ Common cattail

completely fill a shallow pond, as they take root around the edge, multiply, advance toward the center of the water from all sides, and eventually rot away to fill the water below.

In recent years, however, the Common cattail has faced tough competition itself. It is being driven from its habitat by a plant called Purple loosestrife (*Lythrum salicaria*), which is native to Asia, Europe, and North America. Many biologists believe that not only will the Common cattail be driven from its habitat, but also many rare species of waterfowl and wildlife that rely on the Common cattail as a source of food and cover from predators that lurk in the water.

Cattails have their uses

Many water-loving animals make cattail marshes their home. For example, ducks and other waterbirds nest and feed among the stems. Mammals such as raccoons and mink and reptiles such as alligators are also common in cattail swamps, feeding on the fish, amphibians, and other small animals swimming around in the water. Large rodents called muskrats love to feed on the roots of cattails, which are rich in

nutritious carbohydrate (starch), and they often heap up the stems to make their large nests. Microscopic algae grow on the submerged leaves of cattails, appearing as a shiny film, colored golden brown, blue-green, or bright grass-green.

People have long used cattails, too. As well as eating the roots, the green, unripe flower spikes, and the tasty young shoots as salad vegetables, they have also used the yellow pollen as an additive in pancake batters and cookie doughs. Cattails are popular as ornamental plants in garden ponds and in dried flower arrangements, and the dried stems are excellent for weaving baskets, mats, and chair seats.

KEY FACTS

● **Name**
Common cattail
(*Typha latifolia*)

● **Range**
From the Arctic Circle to 30 degrees south of the equator, except for central and southern Africa, southern Asia, Australia, and Polynesia

● **Habitat**
Wetlands

● **Appearance**
Tall, reed-like plant, growing up to 8 ft (2.5 m); long, narrow leaves, ⅓-⅗ in (8-15 mm) wide; large, cylindrical female flower spike topped by a feathery light brown or yellow spike of male flowers

● **Life cycle**
Perennial

● **Uses**
Food; ornamental; weaving

● **Status**
Common

◄ *The fruits of the Common cattail are dispersed by the wind. They have a tiny stalk covered with white hairs that help them float on air currents.*

Cave

Imagine if you had to live your whole life in complete darkness, in a cold, dank place deep underground. Well, some animals do just that, and they are well adapted to their unusual lifestyle.

Many animals can be found in the upper reaches of a cave, near the mouth. Large mammals, such as bears, foxes, and lynx, shelter here when they have young or during particularly harsh winters. Bats and birds roost here, feeding on the insects and spiders that live there too. Even humans used to live in caves in prehistoric times.

However, deeper underground, where it is far too dark for green plants to grow, there are only a few, specially evolved cave inhabitants, which live on the bacteria and fungi that thrive there. Termed troglodytes or cavernicoles, these creatures include species of invertebrates, freshwater fish, crustaceans, and amphibians.

Life in eternal darkness

One thing most of these cave-dwelling creatures have in common is an adaptation to a lack of light. The first thing you notice about them is how pale they are. This is due to a lack of a chemical compound in the skin, known as pigment, which absorbs light and gives organisms their color. In a dark cave, coloration is an unnecessary luxury.

The second thing you would notice if you looked very closely is that many of these animals have poor vision – after all, what is the point of having good eyesight if you live in total darkness? Two examples of such pale, sightless animals are cave fish and the amphibian *Proteus anguinus*. These creatures have other ways of finding their way around in the darkness.

Other ways of sensing

There are four species of cave fish (*Amblyopsis* spp.), which grow to around

NATURAL HABITAT

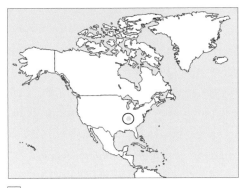

☐ Flint Ridge Mammoth Cave

4 in (10 cm) in length. Although they have eyes, these are extremely small and cannot be used for sight. To make up for this, the fish have touch-sensitive organs covering their whole body, which are stimulated by turbulence in the water. These fish are able to feel their way around the underground pools in which they live.

Also commonly known as the manfish, *Proteus anguinus* is the largest troglodyte that we know of, measuring up to 1 ft (0.3 m) long. It is not a fish but a type of salamander, with a long, thin, streamlined body and tail and four tiny legs. It also has distinctive pink gills protruding from either side of its head. The manfish is totally blind and, like cave fish, relies on touch to feel its way around pools of water it lives in deep underground.

One of the most fascinating things about this animal is that when it makes its home in caves with a temperature above 59°F (15°C), it gives birth to live young; however,

in caves with a temperature lower than this, it lays eggs.

As well as feeling their way around in dark caverns, cavernicoles have evolved other ways of seeing. For example, cave-dwelling bats from the suborder *Microchiroptera* use a type of sonar to help them swoop through caves. Called echolocation, the animals screech high-pitched clicks that bounce off objects in their path to make a kind of sound-map by which to navigate safely. South American oilbirds (*Steatornis caripensis*) use echolocation, too. Like the Southeast Asian Cave swiftlets (*Collocali* spp.), oilbirds also have touch-sensitive whiskers around their beak.

Cave life in danger

Today, more and more humans are venturing into the world's great cave systems. Some of these are speleologists (speleology is the scientific study of caves), while others are cavers – members of the public who enjoy the danger of exploring caves far underground. In some places, this is having a dramatic effect on cave life, which is often very susceptible to human disturbance.

◀ *A South American oilbird nests in the roof of a cave in Trinidad in the West Indies.*

See also **Bacteria, Bat, Bear, Fox, Fungus, Lynx, Spider**

Chameleon

Chameleons are weird looking lizards, with bulging eyes, a hunched back, and a long curling tail. Most species (scientists have identified over 80 different types of chameleon) live in tropical forests in India, Africa, and Madagascar.

Smart hunters

From head to tail, chameleons are adapted for searching out and catching food and for disguising themselves from enemies. Their bulging eyes swivel independently to give them good, all-around vision. However, when they are looking for insects (or even small mammals) to eat they can turn both eyes to look forward, giving them binocular (two-eyed) vision, which helps them to judge distances.

◀ *This chameleon, sitting in the leafy shade, is a soft green color. However, as soon as it moves into a more sunny position, basking on stones or sand, for example, it turns to a yellow-brown color. And if it is alarmed, its skin may turn completely black.*

When they have focused on their target, they shoot their tongues out to stun and trap unsuspecting prey. Then they roll them up again, just as fast, with the insect inside. In some species, the tongue is as long as the head and body put together.

Chameleons' feet and tails are perfectly adapted to enable them to stalk their prey. Each foot has five toes, but some of the digits have grown together to form pincer-like claws, which can clasp the branches and twigs they climb along. The muscles in their legs are well controlled, so they can keep absolutely still or move incredibly slowly, making it difficult for both predators and prey to see them.

A useful tail

They let their coiled tails hang down from the branch, making them very steady on their feet. Some chameleons sway gently as they grip the branch and, with their upright, flattened bodies, they look like leaves wafting in the breeze.

If enemies do enter into a chase, chameleons are very fast and agile. Their tails act as a fifth limb — they can curl them around branches for extra support. (Some species, known as stump-tailed chameleons,

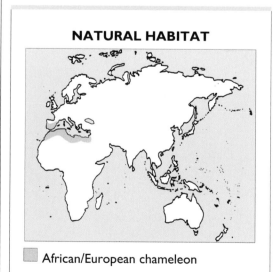

NATURAL HABITAT

African/European chameleon

KEY FACTS

● **Name**
African or
European chameleon
(*Chamaeleo
chamaeleon*)

● **Range**
Africa, north of the
Sahara; some
European and Asian
countries bordering
Mediterranean Sea

● **Habitat**
Warm (but not dry)
grasslands and
tropical forests

● **Appearance**
10 in (25 cm) long,
including a tail;
tongue can reach to
8 in (20 cm); yellow-
brown with darker
stripes, turning green

● **Food**
Insects, spiders,
scorpions

● **Breeding**
Female lays about
30 soft-shelled eggs;
little parental care

● **Status**
Rare

▶ *Curled up inside the
chameleon's mouth is
a long tongue with a
clubbed end covered
in sticky mucus. It uses
it to catch its prey
from a safe distance.*

live on the ground. They have no need of a long tail, but they have the same pincer-like claws as other chameleons, which make them rather clumsy.)

Color coordinated

The most spectacular feature of the chameleons' disguise is their ability to change color. In common with other reptiles, chameleons have scaly, dry skin. They spend much of their time basking in the sunlight or resting in the shade, to keep their body temperature at a fairly constant, comfortable level. Their skin responds to changes in temperature and in a few minutes they can change subtly so that they maintain their camouflage against either a green or a brown background. Some species can change rapidly from display coloring (which they use to attract mates) to complete camouflage coloring. As their bodies change in temperature, so their skins change color. In some species, this may involve a very dramatic change – from black to white.

Some chameleons are territorial, the males establishing a territory for feeding and breeding, and fighting off other males who try to move in on them. When angry they may change color, and some species can inflate themselves, puffing up their skin so that they appear much larger than they are. This technique is also used to frighten off their predators – small mammals, birds, and other reptiles.

Over much of their range, there is little change in the weather from one season to another, so chameleons are able to breed throughout the year. Most female chameleons lay eggs with parchment-like shells, digging out crevices in trees where the eggs hatch and the hatchlings are left to fend for themselves.

The female is able to carry the male's sperm for some time before it penetrates her eggs. Most species lay the eggs eventually, but in one or two pygmy species the female carries the eggs inside her body until they are ready to hatch, so that she actually bears live young.

Chamois

The chamois is a ghost-like inhabitant of European mountains. Like a spirit, it slides silently into view, and then is gone when you blink. It trots gracefully and sure-footedly along the steepest, highest crags and can move like lightning, leaping 6 ft (2 m) upwards or to the side when it wants to escape danger. But although it has the elegance of an antelope, it is in fact part of the goat family.

Getting a foothold

The chamois makes its home in wild, mountainous surroundings, where the weather is harsh and the terrain unwelcoming. However, it has adapted to life in this cruel environment and thrives there. Its feet have become perfectly adapted to moving around craggy rocks that are not only steep in themselves but often covered in ice. The inside of its hoof is elastic and able to grip hard

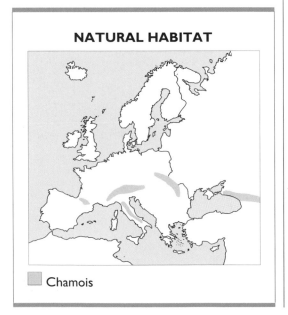

NATURAL HABITAT

☐ Chamois

surfaces, but the outside has a thin, hard layer that can resist the buffetings of leaping around the rocks. In addition, the front of the hoofs point downwards, so that the chamois can keep its footing on the ice, and the hoofs can splay out to allow it to brake on steep hills.

Then, the very shape of the chamois adds to its mountaineering abilities: its body is not very long in relation to its height, so it is very well balanced and able to put all four feet onto a tiny area the

▲ *In order to resist the fierce winter cold, the chamois has a shaggy coat with two layers to provide insulation. The color helps the chamois to hide, as it is blackish-brown with white patches, imitating the colors of rocky slopes with snow on them.*

▲ *The chamois is agile and surefooted. It has a slender, well-balanced body, and leaps nimbly down steep and treacherous mountainsides.*

size of a pocket handkerchief and still retain its balance.

Even the birth of a chamois kid is a mountaineering event. The mother leaves the herd she has been traveling with during the winter to find an isolated rocky outpost where predators such as eagles or wolves will find it difficult to venture, and there she gives birth, normally to a single kid, in late spring.

As soon as the baby chamois has begun to walk (and to imitate its mother's

leaping), the mother rejoins the herds of chamois. During the summer, they spend their time on alpine hills and meadows where they eat by foraging mainly on alpine flowers and wild berries. Then, during the winter, they move further down the mountainside where they begin to browse on vegetation such as lichens, mosses, and pine shoots.

Fight and surrender

Although the chamois appears gentle and graceful, competition between males is aggressive and may result in serious injury or death. Both sexes sport horns that may grow to 1 ft (30 cm) long, and the males use these as weapons in fights to establish territorial dominance.

When a male gets on top in a fight, his foe had better yield immediately by lying down in a posture of surrender; for if the winning male is not placated, he will try to hook his horns into the underbelly of his rival, and such wounds are often fatal.

Although it is so well adapted to living in mountains and to escaping from its natural foes, the chamois has been hunted mercilessly by humans, partly because of its meat but mainly because of its skin, which provides a smooth, hardwearing cloth known as "shammy" leather. Bristles from the winter coat were also prized adornments for hunters.

Now there are scattered populations in southern European mountain ranges but some of these, especially those in the Caucasus, are developing different features (such as differently colored coats) and some experts think they should be treated as separate species.

KEY FACTS

● **Name**
Chamois
(*Rupicapra rupicapra*)

● **Range**
European mountain ranges: Alps, Apennines, Pyrenees, Tatra, Carpathians, Caucasus

● **Habitat**
Steep craggy slopes and Alpine meadows in summer; moves down to more sheltered woodland in winter

● **Appearance**
Length of head and body 40 in (1 m), with a short tail; height at shoulder 30 in (75 cm); slender, hook-shaped horns are carried by both sexes; in winter, the coat is blackish brown, with white patches on the rump and throat; in summer it is yellow

● **Food**
Alpine vegetation including flowers and fruits; mosses, lichens, pine shoots

● **Breeding**
A single kid (rarely 2) is born after a seven month gestation

● **Status**
Endangered over much of its range

Cheetah

The cheetah is a graceful and cunning hunter. Unlike many other meat eaters, such as the leopard or lion, the cheetah depends upon speed rather than brute strength when catching its prey. The fastest animal on land, this elegant cat can reach speeds of over 75 mph (121 km/h). However, it tires quickly and has to limit its running to sprints over short distances.

Built for speed

The cheetah's light body is perfectly adapted for speed, with a slender shape and long legs. Its ability for high speed gives the cheetah an advantage over other hunters in that it can chase after the fastest and most nimble prey. However, its lack of muscle means that it cannot catch many of the larger animals. Another disadvantage is that it is easily attacked and driven away by its competitors – usually other large predators such as lions, leopards, wild dogs, and hyenas.

The cheetah mainly lives in flat, open areas, where rain is scarce. As a result, it has developed the ability to go for long periods without water, surviving on the meat of its prey or sometimes eating juicy desert melons.

The great chase

Taking advantage of its outstanding sight, the cheetah hunts in good light – usually in the morning or late afternoon, and occasionally on very clear moonlit nights. It targets small, light-footed mammals such as gazelles and bushbuck, although sometimes several cheetahs may work together to chase and kill larger antelopes and young zebras.

First the cheetah locates its prey and then stalks it silently, in a low crouch. Once it is as close as possible without being detected, the cheetah breaks into a fast sprint, often pursuing its startled victim for up to 500 yd (460 m).

▼ *The cheetah's back is long and very flexible. It bends up and down as the cheetah runs, giving it a lengthy stride of up to 22 ft (7 m).*

KEY FACTS

- **Name**
  Cheetah
  (*Acinonyx jubatus*)

- **Range**
  Africa, Arabia, Iran

- **Habitat**
  Open savannah, dry grasslands, desert

- **Appearance**
  Long, narrow body measuring 4-5 ft (1-1.5 m) with a tail of 2 ft (0.6 m); small rounded head, short ears, and long legs; golden fur with small black spots, a short coarse mane, black marks on each side of the face from the front of the eye to the mouth

- **Food**
  Medium-sized mammals such as gazelles and impalas; medium-sized birds such as guinea fowl and bustards

- **Breeding**
  Usually between 2 and 4 cubs that are weaned at 3 months and leave their mother at 14-20 months

- **Status**
  Endangered

Making the kill

Without the strength to wrestle animals to the ground, the cheetah takes advantage of its victim's breathlessness and unsteadiness at high speeds. Drawing alongside, it uses its long leg to swipe sideways, knocking the animal over. Before its victim can recover, the cheetah locks its jaws onto the animal's throat, closing the windpipe with a tight grip, which it holds for 5 to 10 minutes, until the exhausted and breathless animal loses consciousness.

The cheetah usually eats its kill on the spot, although it may drag it into the undergrowth to keep it away from other, larger predators. If it is disturbed, it will not return to its meal.

Lone hunters

Female cheetahs are solitary animals, usually living and hunting alone. However, some males – usually brothers – choose to

▲ *Cheetah cubs stay with their mother until they are at least 14 months old – during which time they are taught all the hunting techniques they need to survive on their own. There is an average of three cubs in each litter.*

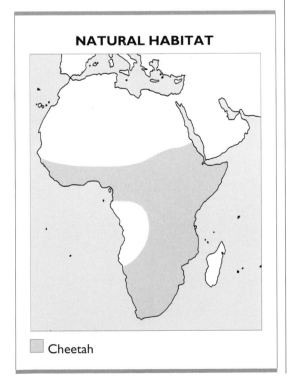

NATURAL HABITAT

☐ Cheetah

live in pairs or groups of three, and work as a team to defend their territory and their mates.

Peaceful and shy animals, cheetahs do not usually fight their rivals and have never been known to attack humans. In the past they have even been tamed and used to help humans hunt in Asia.

Generally, however, cheetahs try to keep away from areas where there are many people, as they are likely to be shot at by farmers. Cheetahs are also suffering from competition with wild dogs and other large cats. There is a shortage of suitable small prey so they have died out in some areas, and their numbers are rapidly decreasing in many others.

See also **Blackbuck**

Chickadee

The chickadees are acrobatic, tree-loving little birds that belong to the titmouse family. Probably the best known of the seven species of chickadee is the Black-capped chickadee, whose call, "Chickadee-dee-dee," leaves little doubt as to how these birds got their name. The Black-cap lives in Alaska, Canada, and in the northern part of the United States and is the state bird of Maine and Massachusetts. It has a gray back and buff sides and pure white cheeks that stand out boldly from the black bib and cap. Male and female look very similar.

A little acrobat

During the winter months, flocks of Black-caps roam woodlands in search of hibernating insects and spiders' eggs to eat. The Black-caps' small size and fantastic agility allow them to hang from

▲ *Perched on a stump, this Black-cap is on the lookout for seeds, berries, and hibernating insects. In winter, they are often seen together with nuthatches, woodpeckers, kinglets, and brown creepers, waiting to dart in to pick up any leftovers.*

the flimsiest of branches to get at food that has been overlooked by other birds. They are also partial to seeds and berries, and are common visitors to gardens and backyards where they will enjoy a meal of suet or sunflower seeds at the feeding station. And, if you are prepared to be patient, Black-caps can become tame enough to take food from the hand.

Cavity nesters

When spring arrives, the chickadees' way of life changes. The flocks start to break up and males and females pair up (usually with the same partner as the previous year) and fly off to breed.

Like other chickadees, Black-caps nest in holes. Both sexes share the task of digging out the nesting cavity and shun ready-made holes. Yet, Black-capped chickadees have been known to accept birdhouses, provided they are filled with wood chips or something similar, so that they can "dig them out" first.

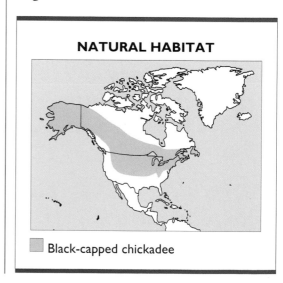

NATURAL HABITAT

Black-capped chickadee

Once the cavity is hollowed out, the female lines the nest with soft material, such as moss and animal fur, and lays a clutch of five to eight eggs. She then sits on them for about two weeks while her mate collects the food for both of them. At the end of this incubation period the eggs hatch, and for the next two weeks or so both parents supply a seemingly never-ending stream of insects to the hungry young birds. When this period is up the young leave the nest but still rely on their parents for food for another week.

After this, the parents are free to raise another brood. Black-caps normally raise a maximum of two broods in a season, but it is highly unlikely that all of the young will survive into adulthood. Many will die of natural causes and others will fall victim to predators such as hawks and the Northern shrike. If they survive youth, they have been recorded as living for as long as eight years in the wild.

Chickadee relatives

The mountains of southwest Canada and the western United States are home to the Mountain chickadee, which looks very similar to the Black-cap but has distinctive white eyebrows. This remarkable little bird, which has been found as high up as 12,500 ft (3810 m), tends to migrate in winter to lower altitudes where it is warmer and food is more plentiful. The Chestnut-backed chickadee also lives in western North America, while the northern forests are home to the Boreal chickadee (which lives in trees) and the Gray-headed chickadee. The latter, the most northern of the

chickadees, was originally an Old World bird and is also known as the Siberian tit.

In the southeastern states, the Carolina chickadee takes the place of the Black-cap. Although these are different species and look and sound slightly different, they have been known to breed together and produce young.

Wider family

The family that the chickadee belongs to contains some 62 species, spread over Europe, Asia, Africa, and North America, where it also includes titmice, the bushtit, and the verdin. In Europe and parts of Asia, the colorful blue and yellow Blue tit takes the place of the Black-cap. They are a welcome sight, feeding from bird feeders in suburban gardens.

◄ **The Black-capped chickadee uses its short beak to peck out nesting holes in trees and stumps. They do not like to move into ready-made holes such as those left by other birds, or birdhouses put out in gardens.**

KEY FACTS

● **Name**
Black-capped chickadee (*Parus atricapillus*)

● **Range**
Canada, northern U.S.

● **Habitat**
Mixed and deciduous woodland, gardens

● **Appearance**
$4^3/_4$-$5^3/_4$ in (12-14 cm); black cap and bib, white cheeks, gray back, buff sides, white below; female has similar coloring

● **Food**
Insects, seeds, and berries

● **Breeding**
Nests in holes, laying 5-8 eggs, which take around 12 days to hatch; more than one brood per year

● **Status**
Common

See also **Hawk**

Chimpanzee

Chimpanzees are clever and lovable. They are the animal most closely related to humans and are among the most intelligent members of the animal world. They have very large brains for their body size and in captivity, do well in intelligence tests. They can even be taught to use complicated sign language.

Remarkably, these skillful and inventive chimpanzees are one of the few animals to use tools for different tasks. They use sticks and stones as weapons in displays of aggression – against other rival chimpanzees or even against their most feared predator, the leopard!

Chimpanzees smash open tough shells with stones to get at the fruit or nuts inside, and use clumps of half-chewed leaves as effective sponges to soak up

NATURAL HABITAT

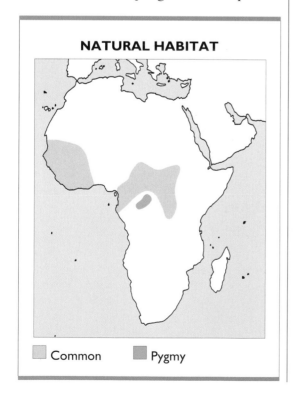

◼ Common ◼ Pygmy

rainwater for drinking. The clever chimps also use grasses and stems to get food, pushing them into holes in termite mounds. When the angry soldier termites clamp on the stems with their jaws, the chimps pull the stems out quickly and eat the termites before they have time to bite.

Living in large groups

Chimpanzees are very sociable and often live in large communities of up to 100

▲ *Chimpanzees' arms are long and powerful, so that they can swing through the lower branches of trees. Mother chimpanzees carry their babies on their backs – even very young chimpanzees are able to cling on tight.*

individuals, chattering to each other with a wide range of sounds and gestures. They are also very clean animals and spend several hours a day in their large groups grooming each other by picking out lice and dirt from their fur or using bunches of leaves to clean themselves. When foraging for food during the day, however, they split up into small groups of two or three – they may even go off on their own when food is scarce.

Teamwork

Despite being so sociable, there is a good deal of rivalry between chimpanzees from different communities; and the males can be extremely ferocious and aggressive, with many fights to the death. However, male chimpanzees often work together to form patrol groups, which travel around their territory, protecting the group from hostile neighbors.

Chimpanzees spend only about a third of their time in the trees – and much of this time is spent sleeping in large nests made from leaves and branches.

About 50 percent of their waking hours are spent feeding. Their diet is mostly made up of ripe fruit, leaves, and insects, although about once a week they

hunt and eat the meat of small mammals such as antelopes, gibbons, and other small monkeys. They may hunt in teams, with each chimpanzee having its own role to play in chasing the prey. Once it is caught, the animal will be torn limb from limb and shared among the group.

The Pygmy chimpanzee

As well as the Common chimpanzee, there is another species called the Pygmy chimpanzee or bonobo (*Pan paniscus*). Despite its name, this species is only slightly smaller than the Common chimpanzee, but it is easily recognizable as it is much darker, with a black face, and spends most of its time in the higher branches of the trees.

The Pygmy chimpanzee is not as widespread as the common species and is only found in an area between the Zaïre river and Kasai river in central Africa.

KEY FACTS

- **Name**
  Common chimpanzee
  (*Pan troglodytes*)

- **Range**
  East, West, and Central Africa, north of the River Zaïre

- **Habitat**
  Humid forests, deciduous woodland

- **Appearance**
  Blackish-brown hair, a short white beard; back sloping down from shoulders to hips; long arms, large hands and feet, large bare ears

- **Food**
  Ripe fruit, nuts, young leaves, insects, small mammals

- **Breeding**
  Usually 1 young born at a time and weaned between 3 and 4 years; females usually remain in the group

- **Status**
  Endangered in wild; threatened in captivity

◄ *This chimpanzee is using a stick to dig for food. Chimpanzee's feet have opposable "thumbs," like those on their hands, which enable them to grip.*

Chipmunk

◀ *The pouches in the chipmunk's cheeks are very stretchy and can expand almost to the size of the chipmunk's head. The chipmunk can tuck up to four large nuts into each pouch.*

KEY FACTS

● **Name**
Eastern Chipmunk
(*Tamias striatus*)

● **Range**
Southeastern
Canada, the eastern
United States

● **Habitat**
Deciduous forests

● **Appearance**
Measures only
$4^{1}/_{2}$-$7^{1}/_{2}$ in
(11-19 cm), with a
relatively long tail of
3-$4^{1}/_{2}$ in ($7^{1}/_{2}$-11cm);
a grayish coat with
dark brown or black
and white stripes
along the body, a
white stripe above
and below each eye,
and a reddish-
brown rump

● **Food**
Seeds, fruit, nuts,
insects, snails,
occasionally eggs and
nestling birds, mice,
and snakes

● **Breeding**
A litter of 2-8
(usually 4 or 5)
young that are blind
and hairless at birth
and weaned at 5
weeks old

● **Status**
Common

Eastern chipmunks are small ground squirrels found mainly in southeastern Canada and the eastern United States. Naturally curious, these mischievous rodents are a common sight in parks – especially at picnic sites where they may try to steal any leftover pieces of food. They are not particularly afraid of humans and are easily tamed.

Eastern chipmunks are active during the day and mostly solitary. They collect their food – seeds, nuts, berries, and insects – from the floor of the forest, where they move about their business with small, quick movements, stopping frequently to look about them for predators such as weasels, bobcats, hawks, and foxes. Occasionally, however, they climb trees and pick the fruit and nuts before they fall. Sometimes they even take eggs and small birds from the nests they find there.

Hoarding supplies for winter

A natural hoarder, the chipmunk gathers any seeds and nuts that it cannot eat on the spot. Sitting upright and holding the food in its front paws, it nibbles away any sharp edges and then places it in the large pouches located in its cheeks. The chipmunk then carries its supplies back to its burrow or various other secure hiding places, where it stores them for winter.

Chipmunks actually spend most of their time underground. They continually add to their burrows throughout their lives, until they have dug out a complex network of tunnels that may extend for more than 30 ft (10 m). There are usually several large chambers within the burrow and many exits – hidden from enemies under tree roots or other ground cover.

An interrupted hibernation

During the cold winter months, the Eastern chipmunk hibernates in its burrow, although it wakes up regularly on warm winter days to eat from its supplies. Using its keen sense of smell to locate its stores, the chipmunk usually finds them easily. However, those seeds and nuts that the chipmunk forgets may go on to sprout and produce new trees and plants for chipmunks to feed on in the future.

▲ *The Asiatic or Siberian chipmunk (Eutamias sibiricus) has sharp claws to help it climb and a long tail to help it to keep its balance as it scampers through the pine trees in search of food.*

Mating occurs during the spring, and the female chipmunk gives birth to a litter of four or five young, the male leaving her to rear them on her own. The young chipmunks are very helpless when they are born, with their eyes closed and no teeth or fur. However, they are almost fully grown after only eight weeks and soon leave their mother to fend for themselves, becoming fully mature at four to six months old.

Many different species

There are 22 different species of chipmunks found in various ranges throughout North America and Asia, including the Least chipmunk (*Tamias minimus*). All of these have very similar habits and look much the same as the Eastern chipmunk, with slight variations according to where they live.

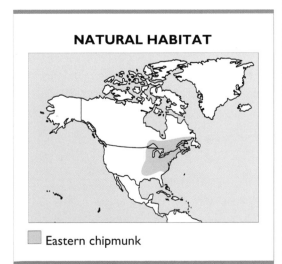

NATURAL HABITAT

Eastern chipmunk

Cicada

The cicadas are well known for their loud and beautiful songs, and there are species found all over the world except in the coldest regions. They are small insects, although the largest of them has a wingspan of 8 in (20 cm).

Common characteristics

Cicadas are classified as bugs – a large group that includes aphids, bedbugs, greenfly, ground pearls, and hoppers (the latter produce frothy "cuckoo spit" when they feed on plants). Scientists define bugs as insects that feed by inserting a long, jointed feeding tube into other animals or plants. Sometimes this can be very unpleasant or even deadly for the victim:

▲ *The adult cicada has delicate wings, with the larger forewings helping to protect the hind wings. It has a fat body and distinctive "bug eyes" almost as big as its head. Its famous and beautiful song is part of its courtship.*

bedbugs, for example, can spread disease between humans, while water boatmen in ponds suck all the vital juices from their victims. Fortunately, the cicadas do not prey on other animals but suck juice from plants or plant roots.

In common with other bugs, cicadas are recognizable by their forewings, which overlap the more delicate hind wings and help to protect them. Something else linking all the bugs is their life cycle.

KEY FACTS

- **Name**
  Cicada
  (*Cicadidae*, a family of 3000 species)

- **Range**
  Worldwide, in tropical and subtropical regions

- **Habitat**
  Woods and forests

- **Appearance**
  Small insects with wingspans of 1-8 in (2.5-20 cm); they have thin, membranous wings; the sucking tube (called a rostrum) points downward

- **Food**
  Sap from vegetation; larvae feed on sap from tree roots

- **Breeding**
  The eggs are laid in trees; they fall to the ground and the larvae burrow down and feed on tree roots until they are developed enough to metamorphose into adults

- **Status**
  Most species are common; destruction of habitat may be dangerous for some

Insects like butterflies undergo complete changes as their eggs hatch into caterpillars, which eventually turn into the adult flying insect. The bugs do not undergo such extreme changes, so that a bug in the early stage of its life, when it is a larva — the equivalent of being a caterpillar — looks, in fact, quite similar to the full adult. This less obvious change in the insect life cycle is known as incomplete metamorphosis.

Slow developers

Although the adult cicada is known for its splendid, sunny song, the young cicadas (the larvae) live in the depths of the earth. The eggs are laid in trees, and when the young hatch they fall to the ground.

At once they begin to dig, using powerful forelegs almost like those of a mole. They are looking for the roots of the tree on which they were born. Once they have found a root, they start to suck the sap from it.

Root sap does not contain much food because it is very watery, thus it often takes cicadas many years to attain full size before they change into adults. In one North American species, this growing process can take as long as 17 years, giving them the name 17-year cicada!

When the cicadas change into adults, they use song to attract mates. It sounds almost like the song of a grasshopper, but it is produced by an entirely different method. Whereas the grasshopper and cricket create sounds by scraping their legs together, the cicada uses muscle power. It has two thin layers of skin (membranes) in the front of its abdomen (the main part of

its body), and a special muscle attached to each of these membranes can suddenly buckle it and then return it to its smooth, resting position. The effect of doing this quickly is rather like clicking the lid of a tin can.

The sound this movement makes is then made louder by air sacs near the membranes so we can hear the songs of some species of cicada at distances of almost a mile (1.5 km).

▲ *These three cicadas are emerging from their larval cases. The cases split open down the back and the pale adult comes out. It is open to attack at first because it cannot fly, but soon it turns a darker color and is able to use its wings.*

See also **Beetle, Butterfly, Moth**

Cinchona

Cinchona is an evergreen tree found in the Andes Mountains, running down South America from Peru to Colombia. It is of particular importance to humans, because its bark contains a substance that can be used to prevent and treat the deadly tropical disease malaria. This disease is caused by a number of microscopic parasites (*Plasmodium* spp.) in the blood. It is spread by female mosquitoes (*Anopheles* spp.), which transfer infected blood from person to person whenever they bite. Every year, malaria affects between 200 and 300 million people in tropical and subtropical regions.

Peruvian countess powder

The medicinal properties of cinchona bark were first discovered by the Peruvian Indians, when they chewed it after watching the same bark-chewing behavior in sick pumas. Then, in 1638, it became known to the Europeans when it was successfully used to treat the Condesa Chinchón, wife of the then Spanish governor of Peru. The tree was named cinchona in her honor, and the medicinal bark was introduced into Europe, where it was also known as Peruvian bark and countess powder. However, it was not until 1820 that the miracle substance, now known as quinine, was isolated from the bark by French pharmacists Pierre-Joseph Pelletier (1788-1842) and Joseph-Bienaimé Caventou (1795-1877) and developed into an antimalarial drug.

From the 1920s onward, several synthetic rivals to quinine came on the market. However, as the *Plasmodium* parasites have developed a resistance to

◄ *These cinchona trees are being cultivated in Senegal, West Africa. Plantations are necessary to prevent overharvesting of trees that are found growing naturally in the Andes Mountains of South America.*

these, quinine has become popular once again. In addition to its medicinal properties, quinine is also used to flavor tonic water.

As well as quinine, cinchona trees also yield other medicinal substances, such as quinidine and cinchonine. All these compounds – known collectively as alkaloids – can be used to treat fever, pain, influenza, and heart problems.

Today, to prevent overharvesting and extinction of the plants, cinchona trees are also cultivated on large plantations in Jamaica, Sri Lanka, India, Malaysia, Java, West Africa, and Australia.

Madder family

There are around 40 species of cinchona tree, four of which are used for the quinine in their bark (Ledger bark, *Cinchona ledgeriana;* Red bark, *Cinchona succirubra;* Brown or Loxa bark, *Cinchona officinalis;* and Yellow bark, *Cinchona calisaya*). Yellow bark is the one that produces the most quinine. These plants are evergreen trees that grow to about 40 ft (12 m) and have large, oval or elliptical leaves, which grow opposite each other on the twigs. They have clusters of perfumed, yellowish-white or rosy-pink flowers and distinctive colored bark. It is the color of the bark that gives some species their other common name: for example, Red cinchona (*Cinchona succiruba*) and Yellow cinchona (*Cinchona calisaya*).

Cinchona trees belong to one of the largest families in the plant kingdom – the madder family (*Rubiaceae*). The madder family contains over 10,000 different species of flowering tree, shrub, and herb,

which range around the world. Most occur in tropical areas, but there are also some species that grow naturally in temperate regions. One species called goosegrass (*Galium aparine*) even grows in Antarctica. Other popular and well-known members of this family are the coffee plants (*Coffea* spp.) and the decorative Cape jasmine (*Gardenia jasminoides*).

▲ *Cinchonas are members of the madder family, which includes the Gardenia species shown above.*

NATURAL HABITAT

▢ Yellow cinchona

KEY FACTS

● **Name**
Yellow cinchona
(*Cinchona calisaya*)

● **Range**
Andes Mountains

● **Habitat**
Tropical valleys

● **Appearance**
Yellow bark; oval or elliptical leaves up to 12 in (30 cm) long

● **Life cycle**
Perennial

● **Uses**
Flavoring in tonic water; medicine

● **Status**
Becoming rare

See also **Coffee, Mosquito**

Clam

You might think of clams as an ingredient of chowder, or you may have had the chance to dig for them on sandy beaches, wriggling your toes into the sand until you find their hard shells. But these little creatures have some impressive relatives. Some of the Great clams found on the Australian Great Barrier Reef have been there for over a hundred years and measure up to 3 ft (1 m) across.

In technical terms, a clam is a bivalve mollusk. Bivalve means that it has two shells. These are hinged together by muscles so that the clam can open and close up to protect itself.

Big brothers

The Giant clam and other large species (such as the Horse's hoof and Giant fluted clams) are found on the coral reefs of the tropical Indian Ocean and in the Western Pacific. They may rest on the sandy ocean floor, but most anchor themselves in between the branching corals. These large, reef-living clams are an extraordinary sight with their dark, fleshy centers protected by thick shells.

Over the years, barnacles, algae, and other marine animals and plants grow over the outer parts of the shells, creating a thick crust. In the coral reef the water is

▲ *This Giant clam, on the Great Barrier Reef off eastern Australia, is covered in a crust of other living plants and animals. Early explorers were wary of them, because they thought that the clams would be able to bite off a man's foot if they stepped on one while it was open.*

rich in food, in the form of tiny living creatures known as plankton. The clams also feed on microscopic plant life (algae).

In order to extract their food from the water, the clams act as filtering machines. Inside its shell, the clam has a kind of skin that takes in water. While the clam's gills extract the oxygen it needs to breathe, its "stomach" absorbs the nutrition from the microscopic plants and animals. The water around a coral reef is particularly rich in plankton and oxygen, so clams thrive in this habitat. Single-celled plants called zooxanthellae live inside the clams and help them to absorb food.

Sand lovers

Many smaller clams living in cooler waters burrow into the sandy bottom where they are well protected from predators. If you were to lay a clam sideways in the sand at the water's edge, you would see it extend its single, muscular "foot" and burrow into the sand. Here, between the grains of sand, the clam finds the same algae and plankton that its tropical cousins feed on.

Many burrowing clams have a pair of tubes known as siphons that extend up from their burrow to the ocean floor. The clam draws in water, sand, plankton, and algae through one tube; when it has extracted what nutrients it needs, it pumps out the sand and debris through the other one.

In order to breed, the clam releases eggs into the water and either the same clam or a neighboring one releases sperm. If any sperm penetrate the eggs, the eggs develop into larvae before growing their shells and reaching adulthood.

The main danger to clams is from the fishing industry. Clams are popular food all over the world and in the past have been dug up with bulldozers at low tide in some places. However, many species are now protected, and mechanical fishing is banned in many areas. Another danger faced by clams in cold climates is winter storms. Sometimes thousands of clams are washed up on beaches, where they soon freeze and starve to death.

◄ *These Butter clams have been dug up along the shore of New Brunswick in eastern Canada. Many people enjoy eating clams; in order to protect them there are strict controls on the way they are dug up.*

KEY FACTS

● **Name**
Giant clam (*Tridacna maxima* and *T. gigas*)

● **Range**
Tropical Indian Ocean and western Pacific Ocean

● **Habitat**
Coral reefs

● **Appearance**
Up to 3 ft (1 m) across; a dark, fleshy "body" protected by an interlocking shell, often encrusted with plants and animals

● **Food**
Plankton, algae

● **Breeding**
Eggs and sperm are released into the water; larval stage, with no parental care

● **Status**
Threatened; protected in Australian waters

NATURAL HABITAT

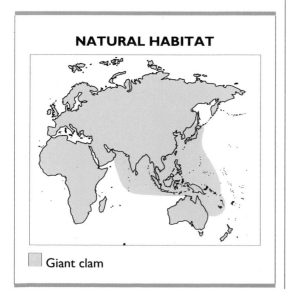

Giant clam

See also **Coral, Coral reef habitat**

Club moss

Club mosses live in cool, damp habitats in many different parts of the world. They are generally small, moss-like, evergreen plants. Although in tropical regions club mosses may reach a height of more than 5 ft (1.5 m), most species grow in a temperate climate and grow no higher than 1 ft (0.3 m). However, club mosses have not always looked like this. More than 300 million years ago, during the Carboniferous Period, the ancestors of club mosses covered most of the Earth and grew into huge trees, over 100 ft (30 m) high. Along with many other plant inhabitants of the great Carboniferous forests, club moss remains, subject to intense pressure for millions of years, form the beds of coal that we mine for fuel today.

There are around 380 species of club mosses (*Lycopodium* spp.), which belong to the plant division *Lycophyta,* along with the spike mosses and the quillworts. All these plants are close relatives of the ferns and, together with horsetails, fork ferns, and whisk ferns, are known as the fern allies.

Structure and appearance

Club moss is not a true moss in that it has stems and roots, with specialized tissue for transporting water and nutrients. Plants that have this kind of tissue are called vascular plants. Club mosses also have

▲ *Ground pine (Lycopodium obscurum) is a small, tree-like club moss, which reaches a maximum height of around 10 in (25 cm). Its small size and needle-like leaves make this plant a popular Christmas decoration. However, many club mosses are becoming endangered as a result of their ornamental value.*

narrow leaves arranged in tight whorls or spirals. Many species have tiny, needle-like leaves and small cones, known as strobili, clustered at the tip of the stem. These make the plants look like miniature Christmas trees.

The stem of most species of club moss creeps along the ground, sometimes under the soil itself, every so often producing low-growing, upright branches. For example, running pine, or Stag's horn moss (*Lycopodium clavatum*), has a stem measuring around 10 ft (3 m) in length and many small branches growing to 4 in (10 cm) in height. In the tropics, however, some club mosses are epiphytes, growing on rocks and trees, which they climb over in their attempt to get closer to the light at the top of the forest canopy. (Unlike parasitic plants, epiphytes use other plant species for support rather than nourishment.)

Flowerless plants

Like their close relatives the ferns, club mosses do not produce seeds for reproduction. Instead, they have a complex, alternating life cycle. All club mosses have special leaves known as sporophylls, with tiny kidney-shaped structures called sporangia. Both the

KEY FACTS

- **Name**
  Ground pine
  (*Lycopodium obscurum*)

- **Range**
  North America and eastern Asia

- **Habitat**
  Damp woods, edges of swamps, and mountainous areas in southern regions

- **Appearance**
  Creeping underground stems, with upright branches reaching a height of around 10 in (25 cm); small, cone-like strobili at the tips of the growing stem

- **Life cycle**
  Perennial

- **Uses**
  Oil from the spores has been used to coat pills; ornamental and decorative, especially at Christmas

- **Status**
  Rare

▶ *Many club mosses are small, evergreen plants. They also have small, needle-like leaves, which are arranged in tight whorls and spirals.*

strobili and sporangia house numerous minuscule spores, which are the reproductive cells. At this stage of the life cycle, the club moss is called a mature sporophyte. When the tiny, pyramid-shaped spores are released, they are carried off by the wind. If their eventual landing place is suitable, fertilization takes place. An ideal place to land is water – fertilization depends on water to enable the reproductive cells to move. The spores germinate and develop into new club mosses, at which point the club moss is known as the gametophyte generation.

Meet the family

Club mosses are part of a larger group of plants within the ferns and allies. They are related to two other families – the quillworts (*Isoetes* spp.), which comprise about 150 species, and the spike mosses (*Selaginella* spp.), which form a larger genus of about 700 species. Club mosses, quillworts, and spike mosses are collectively called the *Lycopsida*.

Using club mosses

Club mosses have had many uses for people through the years. One of the most dramatic features of club mosses is the blinding flash that is produced when the spores are set alight, due to the exceptionally high oil content in the

NATURAL HABITAT

☐ Ground pine

spores. This was capitalized on by manufacturers of the first photographic flashlights and in stage explosives in the theater. The spores have also been used as medicine. They were ground into a powder to stop bleeding – from wounds, nosebleeds, and during childbirth. Some native Americans used it as a talcum powder for their babies. More recently, the spores have been used to coat pills.

Club mosses are also popular as ornamental house and garden plants – too popular. Thus many club moss species are now also endangered or threatened.

See also **Fern, Horsetail, Moss, Quillwort, Whisk fern**

Cobra

Cobras are extremely poisonous snakes that are found in Africa, India, and Southeast Asia. They belong to the group of snakes known as the elapids, which have fangs at the front of their mouths. This group includes North American coral snakes and tree-dwelling African mambas.

Hooded hunters

The King cobra (or hamadryad), the Indian cobra, and the Egyptian cobra are among the better known species. Like all cobras they can raise the front part of their body off the ground and flatten their neck into a "hood" by extending the long, movable ribs that lie behind the head. As the ribs expand they stretch the loose skin of the neck, just as the ribs stretch the cloth of an umbrella when you open it.

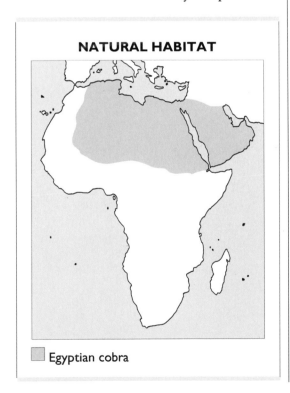

NATURAL HABITAT

☐ Egyptian cobra

The Indian cobra (also known as the Hooded or Spectacled cobra), which is much sought after by snake charmers, has a whitish pattern on the back of its hood.

Cobras raise their body and show off their hood when they are alarmed or excited. It is a warning before they strike their prey; at the same time they hiss and sway their head from side to side. When they strike, they move their head forward and downward, piercing the victim's skin with the two fangs that lie in the upper jaw. The cobra's poison, or venom, is contained in venom glands situated behind the eyes. At the moment the snake strikes, muscles in the head contract to release the venom. The venom passes from the glands into special channels

▲ *The Egyptian cobra has been identified as the asp whose bite was used by Cleopatra VII, queen of Egypt, to commit suicide.*

called ducts running down the back of each fang. The bite of the cobra can be fatal to humans if sufficient venom gets into the victim and if antivenom is not given, or if it is given too late. However, the cobra is really only interested in attacking animals that are small enough to eat whole. It will only attack larger animals – including humans – if it is alarmed or frightened.

The poison of the cobra affects the nervous system and can cause paralysis as well as nausea, breathing difficulties, and, in severe cases, heart failure.

Lifestyle

Cobras live in both open country and in forests. They are ground dwellers that feed on rodents, particularly rats, and on frogs, toads, and birds, although some species climb trees. When food is scarce they will supplement their diet with grasshoppers and other large insects. The King cobra feeds on other snakes and at times even eats young King cobras.

Some cobra species, such as the Egyptian cobra, are active during the day; others are active at night. The nocturnal habits of the Indian cobra are in part responsible for its seemingly "charmed" behavior – rising from its basket at the sound of the music supplied by the snake charmer. The snake is kept in the darkness of the basket until its owner removes the lid. The sudden, bright light alarms the cobra and it rises up and sways in time to the music, seemingly hypnotized by the snake charmer. In fact, the cobra cannot hear the music because it has no eardrums. It is actually watching the snake charmer's flute and following its movements. Raising the front of the body and swaying from side to side is also part of courtship behavior, when male and female "dance" together before mating.

The female lays 8-20 eggs in a hole in the ground or, more rarely, in a tree. When newly hatched, the young are about 10 in (25 cm) long. With the exception of the King cobra, the parents do not look after the eggs or the young. The female King cobra, however, lays her eggs in a nest of leaves, soil, and grass in a hollow in the ground. She then lies on the nest until the eggs hatch. The young snakes shed their skins as they grow; when their skin becomes too tight, they rub their mouth and head against rocks to scrape away the old skin, and then wriggle out of it, revealing a new skin underneath.

▼ *This Spitting cobra can spit venom over a distance of 7 ft (2 m). It aims at the victim's face or eyes. The venom irritates the skin and can cause blindness as well as pain. If spitting does not frighten predators, the cobra will bite.*

KEY FACTS

- **Name**
Egyptian cobra
(*Naja haje*)

- **Range**
Northern and central Africa; Arabian peninsula

- **Habitat**
Deserts, scrublands

- **Appearance**
Up to 6 ft (180 cm) long; brown, overlapping scales, with paler underside

- **Food**
Lizards and rodents

- **Breeding**
Lays 8-20 eggs that do not need incubating, although mother protects eggs against predators

- **Status**
Rare

Cockatoo

Cockatoos are colorful, noisy birds belonging to the parrot family. In Australia and New Guinea, they are often seen flying through the treetops in huge flocks of up to 100, chattering to each other with loud shrieks and squawks. They are very pretty, with bright feathers and attractive crests that stand out against the leaves of the trees. These crests can be raised or lowered at will; the cockatoos usually raise them when landing or if they are alarmed.

There are 18 different species of cockatoo found in open woodland throughout northern and eastern Australia, and tropical forests in New Guinea and its surrounding islands. They range in size from the small, gray cockatiel (*Nymphicus hollandicus*), which measures about $12^1/_2$ in (32 cm), to the large Great black or Palm cockatoo (*Probosciger aterrimus*), which may grow to 32 in (80 cm) long.

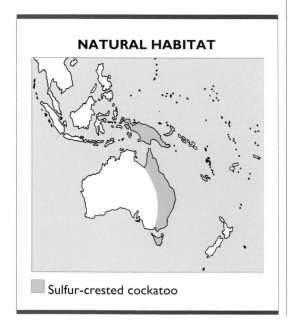

NATURAL HABITAT

Sulfur-crested cockatoo

The different species of cockatoo also vary in color, although most of them are either white or dark gray, with shades of pink or yellow on their crests and faces.

Living in trees

Cockatoos are active during the day and spend the night together in large roosts. At sunrise, they leave these roosts and fly to their feeding grounds nearby. There, much of the day is spent in the trees, where the cockatoos feed on leaves, fruit, and flowers, or the larvae of moths and beetles. However, some species such as

▲ *Cockatoos are closely related to parrots. However, they can be easily told apart by the brightly colored crests that cockatoos have on top of their heads. This cockatoo has a magnificent yellow crest – which gives it its name, the Sulfur-crested cockatoo.*

the cockatiels often descend to the ground in small flocks to forage for grass seeds.

Like other parrots, cockatoos have very powerful, short beaks that are curved downward. The upper part of the beak is hinged and moved by muscles so that it can be used for a wide variety of tasks – such as delicately preening its feathers, powerfully crushing hard nuts or seeds, holding food, or helping the cockatoo climb through the branches of the trees.

Cockatoos also have feet similar to those of parrots, with two outer toes that point backward, and two inner toes that point forward. These allow the birds to grasp the tree branches tightly; they can even hold objects close to their beaks, as if they had hands.

Laying eggs

Breeding seasons vary among the different species of cockatoo; some species will mate at any time of year. Most cockatoos are monogamous (they only have one partner at a time); and many males and females stay together for life, often feeding and preening each other. After a short courtship display, the cockatoos mate and then build a nest in the hollow of a tree high above the ground. The female lays 1-3 eggs (4-7 for cockatiels); and then she or her partner sits on them for up to 30 days until they hatch. The young birds stay in the nest for up to 10 weeks before leaving their parents.

Threats to the cockatoo

Cockatoos are always on the lookout for their enemies – birds of prey such as hawks and falcons, monkeys, and other tree-dwelling mammals that may also steal eggs and nestlings.

However, the biggest threat to most cockatoos is the human exploitation and destruction of tropical forests. By contrast, the Galah or Rose-breasted cockatoo (*Eolophus roseicapillus*) has largely benefited from human settlement in Australia, and it is now the commonest species of cockatoo within its range.

KEY FACTS

● **Name**
Sulfur-crested cockatoo (*Cacatua galerita*)

● **Range**
New Guinea and surrounding islands; Australia

● **Habitat**
Open woodland, tropical forest

● **Appearance**
20 in (50 cm) long from head to tail, with white plumage, a yellow crest on its head, and a black, hooked beak

● **Food**
Seeds, fruit, nuts, flowers, leaves, insects

● **Breeding**
2 or 3 eggs are laid in a hole in a tree and incubated, mainly by the female, for about 30 days; the young birds leave the nest after 6-10 weeks

● **Status**
Common in some areas

◄ *Like other cockatoo species, these Pink cockatoos (Cacatua leadbeateri) are very sociable and like to gather in small flocks.*

See also **Parrot**

Cockroach

The cockroach is an excellent example of a highly successful animal – one that has a remarkable ability to adapt to changing conditions. This ability has ensured its survival over millions of years. Fossil remains of cockroaches prove that many species existed some 345 million years ago and these early insects were very much like those living today. The cockroach is an active insect, usually coming out at night, and different species have many different habits and shapes.

Designed for survival
The typical cockroach has a flattened body and long legs adapted for running, so that it can escape quickly into cracks and crevices when it is threatened. The sense organs (eyes and antennae) on the head are highly developed. The eyes are complex, like a fly's, and are made up of many small tubes. The antennae move about freely and are very sensitive to

▲ The Cape mountain cockroach of South Africa is unusual in that it gives birth to live young. The larvae are like miniature versions of the adult.

touch; they do the work of a nose, smelling the air around them.

There are two pairs of wings: the forewings, which are thick and tough, protect the delicate, membranous hind wings, just as those of beetles. While some cockroach species have lost the hind wings, others such as some of the large, tropical species still use their wings to fly about freely at night. In these insects the hind wings fold up like a fan when they are not in use and expand to provide a large surface area when the insect is in the air. Flying cockroaches are attracted to light and often fly into houses through open windows on hot summer evenings.

Habitats and niches
Cockroaches are found in tropical, subtropical, temperate, and cold regions, in almost every type of habitat including human dwellings. The majority of species, however, live in the wild – practically anywhere where there is plenty of organic matter to provide them with a food supply. Dead and decaying vegetation, growing plants, and carrion are not only sources of food but may also be places where they can shelter.

While most cockroaches are ground dwellers, others burrow beneath the ground or climb high up into trees. An entire family of cockroaches, the *Cryptocercidae* of North America and Asia, feed only on wood. In an outstanding example of adaptation, their digestive systems contain tiny microorganisms that process the wood for them. Without them this would normally be indigestible.

Domestic menaces

In all parts of the world there are cockroaches that live among humans – specifically in places where food is stored or prepared. The "domesticated" species are not as numerous as their wild relatives, but they are detested by humans as household pests. They creep out of their hiding places at night in search of food. They eat any food they come across, both fresh food and garbage, and even things you might not think of as food, such as bookbindings and shoe polish. They not only cause damage, they also carry disease. Cockroaches drop their excrement onto food and leave behind harmful bacteria that they carry on their bodies from germ-ridden areas. Once established, these unhygienic pests are difficult to remove because they hide themselves away in tight corners.

Eggs, nymphs, and adults

Female, egg-laying cockroaches enclose their eggs in a hard capsule known as an ootheca. The female may carry this around with her for a few days before depositing it in a crevice or among debris. An ootheca usually holds about 16 eggs neatly arranged in two rows. When the young have hatched, the ootheca splits to allow them out.

Eggs laid by the female hatch into young that are in most respects smaller, wingless versions of the adult. As the young (called nymphs) develop they become too big for their skin, so they shed it to make way for the new one. This process may be repeated as many as six to 12 times over 10 months to a year.

However, in one species there are no eggs and the young are born live; in several others, the female holds the eggs in a special brood patch on her body until they are ready to hatch so that they seem to be born alive.

KEY FACTS

● **Name**
American cockroach (*Periplaneta americana*) is one of about 3700 species

● **Range**
Found in most parts of the world

● **Habitat**
Many live in towns; species are adapted to almost any environment, from mountains to deserts

● **Appearance**
Medium to large, 1/2-2 1/2 in (1-6 cm) long; long antennae; hard brown forewings

● **Food**
Scavengers, they will eat almost any organic matter

● **Breeding**
Most species lay eggs that hatch into nymphs (small, wingless versions of adults)

● **Status**
Widespread

◄ *This American cockroach has found some tasty cookies, but will leave them covered with germs. Although large, this is not the largest species.*

See also **Beetle**

Coconut palm

The Coconut palm (*Cocos nucifera*) is a member of the palm family (*Arecaceae*). Although no one is really sure where it came from originally, some botanists think the Coconut palm may have come from Polynesia. It is now found growing wild in southern Florida and on shores throughout the tropics. Its ideal habitat is close to the ocean, with a large amount of rainfall, high humidity, and an average temperature of 85°F (29.5°C).

Huge, floating seeds

The key to the Coconut palm's amazing ability to colonize new areas is its fruit. These are the familiar coconuts, one of the largest fruits in the plant world. They are generally 8-12 in (20-30 cm) in length and 8 in (20 cm) in diameter. Inside is a rich, watery liquid called coconut milk and a layer of sweet, white flesh, up to ⅘ in (2 cm) thick. Around this is a hard shell, covered in turn by a fibrous husk. Despite its huge size, the coconut can float in the sea for many miles, taking up to four months to reach its final destination.

NATURAL HABITAT

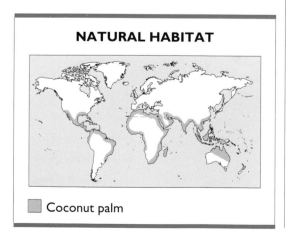

Coconut palm

When a coconut finally washes up on some far-flung tropical beach, it sprouts, sending up a shoot and large, green leaves and sending down deep roots. A giant of the palm family, this seedling may eventually reach 100 ft (30 m) in height, with a crown of leaves, each of which may measure as much as 20 ft (6 m) long. The flowers are borne in inflorescences

▲ *The Coconut palm is often found by seashores and areas close to the coast. Its fruit is waterproof and can float in the sea for many hundreds of miles before reaching land again.*

◄ *The fruit of the Coconut palm has many uses. It contains a nutritious food as well as a rich, watery liquid called coconut milk.*

resembling long, drooping spikes. They are usually pollinated by the wind, but many botanists believe that bees, wasps, beetles, flies, and ants may also be responsible for pollination. Once the flowers have been pollinated and fertilization has occurred, the palm will produce fruit of its own, growing in clusters of between 5 to 20 nuts. These take around a year to ripen and may be red, yellow, green, or brown. The Coconut palm has a characteristic curved trunk, swollen at the base, which leans over the shoreline. As it drops its ripe fruit, the coconuts are washed out to sea by the powerful ocean currents, and the whole cycle begins once again.

Coconut products

People use just about every part of the Coconut palm. The trunk provides useful timber, called porcupine wood, for building houses and furniture; the flowers yield sugar and an alcoholic drink known as palm wine; and the leaves can be woven into mats, baskets, and thatch for the roofs of houses. Even the coconut has more uses than you might think. As well as eating and drinking the nutritious, white meat-like fruit and sweet milk, you can eat the flesh dried (when it is known as copra) or press it for oil for use in cooking or for soap, candles, and other household products. The thick fibers from the outside of the nuts (known as coir) can be used to make ropes and mats. The coconut is such a valuable commodity that most of the world's coconuts are grown on small, native plantations in a variety of tropical countries, such as Sri Lanka, the Philippines, Malaysia, and Indonesia. Under cultivation, each Coconut palm may bear between 50 and 180 coconuts per year until the trees are about 60 years old.

KEY FACTS

● **Name**
Coconut palm
(*Cocos nucifera*)

● **Range**
Throughout the tropics

● **Habitat**
Low-lying areas close to the coast

● **Appearance**
A tall, slender, ringed trunk, swollen at the base, curving slightly and reaching up to 100 ft (30 m); crowned with many large, feather-shaped leaves, measuring 20 ft (6 m) or so in length; mature fruits are oval-shaped, ellipsoid, or ovoid, 8-12 in (20-30 cm) in length, 6-8 in (15-20 cm) in diameter, and covered with thick, brown fibers

● **Life cycle**
Perennial

● **Uses**
Building materials; fiber; food; oil

● **Status**
Widespread

See also **Palm**

Cod

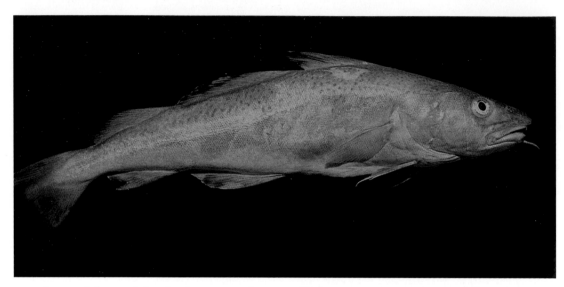

◄ *Cod grow rapidly. At 9 months, they are about 6 in (15 cm) long, doubling their size over the next year. Adults reach 2-3 ft (60-90 cm).*

Members of the cod family live in cool to temperate waters worldwide. They include the Common or Atlantic cod, haddock, hake, ling, whiting, and pollack. All of these fish are caught for their edible flesh and some, such as the Atlantic cod, for the oil produced in the liver. They are therefore of great commercial importance to the fishing industries of North America and Europe.

The Atlantic cod is found in those areas of the northern oceans and seas that have traditionally been fished by trawlers and netters for hundreds of years: the North Sea and the waters off Newfoundland, Labrador, Greenland, Iceland, Norway, and Bear Island.

The areas in which individual cod populations are found are vast and are divided into feeding and spawning (breeding) grounds. The fish may therefore have to travel several hundred miles from one area to another. Atlantic cod, for example, may travel from Iceland all the way to Greenland. Within the feeding areas the fish move from one part to another according to the seasons.

The Atlantic cod feeds in deep waters during the summer; in the fall it moves into shallower waters near the coast to feed on the sea bed.

Many cod species live in schools. They keep in touch with one another by sounds produced in the swim bladder. This is located beneath the backbone and enables the fish to remain at a particular depth.

Voracious feeders

Cod are predatory fish that feed on other fish, shrimps, and other types of sea creatures such as worms. They have enormous appetites and sometimes gorge themselves when food is plentiful. The haddock, for example, will consume herring eggs in such quantities that its stomach becomes crammed with the food. This fish lives mainly on the sea bottom. Its overlapping upper lip is an adaptation

KEY FACTS

● **Name**
Atlantic cod
(*Gadus morhua*)

● **Range**
North Atlantic,
North Sea

● **Habitat**
Lives in deep water
during the summer,
moving to shallower
waters during the
winter

● **Appearance**
4 ft (120 cm)

● **Food**
Crustaceans, small
fish; the young feed
on plankton, larvae,
and eggs

● **Breeding**
The female lays
millions of eggs that
are fertilized
externally; no
parental care

● **Status**
Threatened

to feeding that allows it to scoop up worms, mollusks, and other bottom dwellers from the seabed.

The pollock (also known as the saithe, coalfish, or pollack) feeds on shrimp and young fish (fry). It lives and hunts in schools, with an interesting technique for catching its prey. A school that comes across a group of young fish will completely surround the fry on all sides, driving them into a dense mass. Then, with great speed, the school drives the fish up towards the surface. Once they are near the surface, they attract sea birds on the lookout for food; in the meantime the school of pollack attacks from below.

A varied diet

The Atlantic cod, unlike most of its relatives, does not move in schools, but usually hunts in large groups, particularly when there is plenty of food about. It takes a wide variety of prey, including herring, haddock, mackerel, squid, shrimp, crabs, and worms from the bottom. It has very sharp, pointed teeth and its digestive juices contain chemicals that dissolve the shells of animals such as crabs. This cod also has a reputation for devouring anything, so great is its greed. There have been reports of some surprising items found in the stomach, including a book and a set of keys.

The life cycle of the Atlantic cod is typical of many of the cod family. Once at the spawning grounds the female releases her eggs into the water and the male releases milt (sperm). The eggs rise to the surface, and within 10 to 20 days they hatch into larval fish ¼ in (6 mm)

long. These tiny fish live in the surface plankton for approximately 75 days. When they reach a length of about ¾ in (19 mm) they move to the bottom of the sea at depths of 240 ft (75 m). Here they feed on small crabs and other sea creatures; as they develop they swim into deeper waters.

The eggs and young face many dangers, not least the possibility of being eaten by other fish. Many eggs are not even fertilized and many that are do not hatch. By way of compensation, a female Atlantic cod may shed up to four to six million eggs in one spawning season alone.

In other species the young have found ways of protecting themselves. Young whiting harbor under the "bell" of a jellyfish, gathering among the poisonous tentacles beneath the bell. This gives them protection from larger predators.

▲ *Although female cod lay millions of eggs, there are tight controls on fishing for them to ensure that their numbers do not dwindle.*

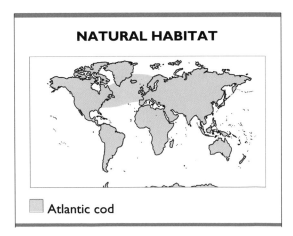

NATURAL HABITAT

Atlantic cod

Coelacanth

The coelacanth is one of many very ancient, primitive fish that flourished on Earth at a time when animals were just beginning to make their way out of the water onto the land. Although many fossils have been found, none has been found in rocks younger than 70 million years. Because of this information, until quite recently scientists believed that the coelacanth had died out.

The living fossil

In one of the most exciting scientific finds of the twentieth century, on December 22, 1938, a trawler fishing off the coast of Natal, South Africa, brought up in its net a large, strange looking fish that the fishermen could not identify. The net had been dragged along the seabed at a depth of 120 ft (36.5 m) and had caught about three tons of known species of fish. The unusual specimen the fishermen had brought to the surface was 5 ft (150 cm)

▲ *A heavy, ungainly fish, the coelacanth takes its name from the supporting spines in the fleshy part of its fins and tail. These are hollow – and the name coelacanth means "hollow spine."*

NATURAL HABITAT

☐ Coelacanth

long and blue, with thick armored scales. The curator of the local museum at East London in Natal, a Miss Courtenay-Latimer, saw the fish and soon after wrote to an expert on African fish, Professor J.L.B. Smith, describing what she had seen. When Professor Smith eventually saw the fish, he correctly identified it as a coelacanth and named it *Latimeria chalumnae* after Miss Courtenay-Latimer.

Following this discovery Professor Smith advertised a reward for anyone who could find him a similar fish. Almost 14 years later, on December 20, 1952, a second coelacanth was caught in the Indian Ocean northwest of Madagascar, off one of the tiny islands of Comoro. Then, between September 1953 and January 1954, three more coelacanths were dragged up from the ocean in a search conducted in the area by French scientists. Since then some 100 other individuals have been caught, all of them in the tropical waters of the west Indian Ocean. It is now apparent that the first specimen known to western science, caught off South Africa, had somehow wandered a long way from its normal habitat.

The first and many subsequent coelacanths taken from the Indian Ocean were caught on lines by native fishermen of the Comoros. Unlike scientists in the western world, these fishermen had known of the existence of the living coelacanth for years beyond memory.

The peculiarities of a peculiar fish

The coelacanth lives in deep waters at depths of some 220 ft (67 m), especially in those places where the seafloor takes a sudden plunge, creating a vertical wall that drops into darkness. It is a heavy fish, weighing up to 200 lb (90 kg) and growing to a length of 6 ft (1.9 m). It has several external features that are only seen in this species, including bony-plated scales covered with small, tooth-like points. The tail is also unique in living species. It is divided into two equal parts by the tapering, rear end of the body, creating in fact a "double" tail that acts like a paddle when the fish swims. This links the coelacanth with the primitive Rhipidistian fish that lived about 320 million years ago and which are thought to be the ancestors of land animals.

A third peculiarity of the coelacanth is the fact that the pectoral (side) fins are set on a muscular lobe that works rather like a limb. This enables the fish to twist its fins and move them back and forth. The pectoral fins are probably used to maneuver the fish along the seabed as it searches for prey. The spines of the fins are made of soft, bone-like cartilage and are hollow.

The whole body is covered in a slimy substance, and the muscles and head hold large amounts of oil. The skull is hinged, as it is in the fossil coelacanths; the brain is small compared to the large cavity in which it sits.

Living young

A young fossil coelacanth unearthed in rocks in Illinois has remnants of the yolk sac underneath it. For years scientists debated whether this meant that the coelacanth actully gave birth to live young, rather than laying eggs. Eventually a female coelacanth specimen in the American Museum of Natural History was dissected, revealing five young fish that had been near birth when the female died.

Study of live coelacanths has been almost impossible as those that have been captured so far have survived for only a few hours. They appear to be unable to survive in warm, shallow waters and probably also suffer from the change of pressure as they are lifted from the ocean's depths. Catching and landing a coelacanth is difficult because of the weight and bulkiness of the fish.

▼ *Fossil coelacanths like this one, measuring about 6 in (150 mm), have been found in rocks between 450 and 70 million years old.*

KEY FACTS	
● **Name**	Coelacanth (*Latimeria chalumnae*)
● **Range**	West Indian Ocean
● **Habitat**	Tropical waters at depths as low as 220 ft (67 m)
● **Appearance**	Up to 6 ft (1.9 m) long; dark brown to blue, sometimes with light flecks on the scales; strong pectoral fins and a double tail
● **Food**	Fish
● **Breeding**	Gives birth to live young; gestation may last 12 months
● **Status**	Endangered

Index

Page numbers in **boldface** type show full articles